THERE'S ONLY
ONE
OF US HERE

THERE'S ONLY
ONE
OF US
HERE

A GUIDE FOR ASPIRING LIGHTSEEKERS

DAVID DIPIETRO WEISS

River Sanctuary
PUBLISHING

First Edition
ISBN 978-1-935914-07-5

Design by Jessica Moreno

Printed in the United States of America

To order additional copies please visit:
www.spiritualpathfinder.com

RIVER SANCTUARY PUBLISHING
P.O Box 1561
Felton, CA 95018
www.riversanctuarypublishing.com
Dedicated to the awakening of the New Earth

THIS BOOK IS dedicated to the memory of my mother, Elena Margharita DiPietro (Helen), whose old world philosophy of *Sweep Your Own Porch First* resonated within my soul and enabled me to go within myself to establish my true soul identity while allowing all others the non-judgemental epithet of — *They Get To Do That!* Her dedication and love for me was constantly on display for my entire life. Bless her!

And

To my father, Fred Weiss, a salt-of-the-earth, hard-working man who could never conjure a bad word for anyone; who was there when I needed him; and who would give anyone his last dollar, his generous time, or his most prized possession — coupled with a warm smile and greeting while expecting nothing in return. Bless his soul! The world needs more men like him.

And

With pride, I take the middle name DiPietro to co-honor my mother and her family whose last male passed leaving the name to end in time and space, yet *never* in spirit.

With love and sweet memory of generations past, Namaste!

David DiPietro Weiss

As with any project, there are many others who contribure to its production. First and foremost, many thanks to my beautiful spouse, Annie Elizabeth, for her countless contributions assisting me in correlating my spiritual thoughts and writing.

- To Adra Ross, who was my first critical reader of the original manuscript and graciously helped me re-direct my writing process.

- To Jessica Moreno, my lovely and talented daughter-in-law, whose undying dedication in laying out the book format and designing the cover was truly a gift of love.

- To Markos Moreno, my stepson, whose initial forays into book cover design were instumental in finalizing the product.

- To all those in our spiritual seminar groups who reflected their thoughts, feelings, and spirit that contributed mightily to the final product.

- And, of course, to Rumi, my 4 year old German Shepherd, who adoringly sat aside me during some tedious writing and rewriting sessions.

- Thanks to all for helping to make this book a reality.

CONTENTS

PREFACE

Who Made You?
   God made you.
Who is God?
   God is the Supreme Being who made all things.

AND SO THE systematic religious training of new and young Catholics begins. It is a process by catechism,[1] a handbook of questions and answers with which the church teaches and indoctrinates her new disciples in the ways and tenets of the Catholic faith while assuring that each new disciple comprehends the story of creation and interpretation of divine law as perceived by the church's spiritual leaders. As a young boy, I remember succinctly the tedium of memorizing my lessons so I wouldn't be scolded for not being able to respond correctly to my instructor/priest. After all, I was an excellent student and didn't want to mar that image or disappoint my priests. When finally, during confirmation by the regional Bishop as a Catholic, I sat in the church fearful that the Bishop, another intimidating Catholic persona in the hierarchy of the Catholic Church, resplendent in his officious garb, would ask me a question I couldn't answer well. He didn't. It was a lesson though in fear-based learning and served to greatly influence my later career as an educator. I vowed I would never present learning where my students would be intimidated by my authority or personality. Nor would I accept a spiritual doctrine that was based on fear and blind acceptance.

For many, the process of catechism is a very effective method of teaching the young. As children, we learn and easily accept when a figure introduced as a holy and commanding priest—a respected and recommended teacher—further encouraged and facilitated by one's parents, teaches us the meaning of life and the hereafter. The catechism process is, and has been, a useful tool for the church to simplify the teachings of Catholicism. Once we, as students, accept the basic premise of the teaching, the rest of the potential dogma follows that basic thought. We are not encouraged to think or act beyond the teachings of the church and, indeed, to attend any other service or give credence to thoughts that were contrary to the teachings of Catholicism.

Accordingly, but to avoid indoctrination, *There's Only One of Us Here* is presented in a catechism-like format of questions and answers—certainly without the accompaniment of intimidation and fear factors. I introduce this book as a primer, an opening path for aspiring *Lightseekers*, (folks like you and me—indeed—who are on a path to spiritual knowledge—irrespective of our religious training or spiritual upbringing.)[2] In this book it is my desire to invite the reader to consider basic spiritual questions while building a foundation of thought to better understand, grapple with, and gain new comprehensions pertaining to the ancient and historical teachings about spirit. We will examine topics such as who we are and how we got here, who or what is God, along with a host of companion inquiries such as our purpose, the roles of ego, forgiveness, gratitude, meditation, prayer, free will, intention and affirmations. In today's consciousness, we will also take a peek at the mysterious world of quantum physics.[3]

Let's begin by exploring some basic world-wide concepts of spirituality and religion: the multiple spiritual paths, the evolution of spiritual awareness, the importance of living in the NOW, our innate ability to create our life, and the definition of God. It can be quite a journey.

The curiosity to explore the tenets of the varied religions and spiritual pursuits is essential to the understanding of the spiritual basis of our world being. Each religion is prized by its devotees as each group gives every individual spiritual instruction on how to live and to worship God. All religions are valuable and valued and there is no reason why any one of us should devalue another's peaceful path to God. Recognizing that such diverse paths exist, one can welcome any pursuit that chooses God as its moral precept and offers practices that enhance our lives with love, peace, tolerance, and joy. It is my belief that any peaceful spiritual path that one chooses will be the right path for each individual in his or her current space in time.

I honor all who pursue a spiritual foundation and loving practice for their lives and wish them well on their divine pursuit. Each of us has the ability and the right to define and practice our own path to the divine. Kahlil Gibran says it well:

Say not, I have found the path of the soul, say rather, I have met the soul while walking on my path.[4]

One of my own favorite personal statements concerning beliefs and practices of the myriad of religions is, *"They get to do that"*—a very simple avowal of tolerance, appreciation, understanding and non-judgment. We all *get* to create our unique path, our God, as discovered and recognized in our deepest intuitive knowing. Other folks get to do their thing. The key to an appropriate attitude regarding what others do lies within each of us. As observers of one another, the choices we make to respond to the beliefs and practices of others presents the opportunity for us to judge or not judge and to appreciate and tolerate, or not. Each life situation gives us the opportunity to recognize what is, not what we wish was—without the burdening judgment we tend to insist upon. It follows that *"they get to do that"* because there is very little, if anything, we can do to change what they think. We have enough to do ourselves and deal with our own chatterbox *"monkey mind"* than spending our energy trying to "fix" others.

Often, because we are human, we tend to give God an anthropomorphic image to connect ourselves to our Source. As a result of our teaching, we often picture the Christian God as a white-bearded, elderly man who occupies a jeweled throne somewhere in our concept of heaven. As such we tend to identify God as having many of the same physical attributes as ourselves. We thus create our image of God that reflects our human qualities. Voltaire, the French writer & philosopher (1694-1778) said, "God created man in his own image and man promptly returned the compliment." In the same era (1689–1755), philosopher Montesquieu wrote, "If triangles had a God, God would have three sides." Voltaire and Montesquieu would have agreed on man's reflections.

As a young boy I questioned the image of God as taught by the priests. My still developing mind could not contemplate an image of heaven where angels flew around in the clouds playing harps. What kind of God would call that paradise? There must be some other explanation, I thought. I knew that one day I might find a more appropriate answer.

As I matured and grew older (there is a difference!) I realized that not only are there numerous and diverse spiritual paths that exist, but that our spiritual awareness as a species is also evolving.

Science, for example, always develops new thought and thinking processes by correcting itself as it goes along. Consequently, science constantly updates facts and assumptions as it evolves and embraces new knowledge. And so it should be with man's spiritual pursuits. As we learn more and more about ourselves, our human and spiritual potential, our relationships with the environment, with family, friends, flora and fauna, and the universe, we can choose to reexamine and/or reinvent ourselves according to new information, new insights and deeper revelations. Our new realizations and connections to the universal truth and acknowledgement of our Source and Spirit selves leads us to reexaminations, reinterpretations, new knowledge and celebrations of the NOW.

Let's take a moment and reintroduce ourselves to the NOW. For many in this new millennium, there is the realization that our lives are intrinsically bound together as one and that we only have the NOW—this moment. There is only the NOW. The past is gone forever. It cannot necessarily be changed in this earthly existence. The future is but a vision created by *choices* we make in the NOW. Therefore, there is only the NOW that truly exists. How we live, love, and conduct ourselves is a continual series of *choices* for us in the NOW, this moment. We can *choose* to create as we live. What we *choose* to see, and how we *choose* to feel, creates our reality. Our *thoughts* manifest our realities for all of us as individuals, and as the whole. In truth, we can *choose* to acknowledge, or not, that there is only one of us here as we are all connected to one another. Amazing science and inspiration has allowed us, as we seek verification of these phenomena, to approach spirit from a new perspective. The relatively new science of quantum physics reveals and demonstrates the power that thought has over what we experience as substance.[4] Indeed, at the molecular level, all substance, living or seemingly inert, including animated us, is composed of atoms in various vibrations. How they are arranged and vibrate together is subject to how we choose to think about them.

The great Indian sage, Mahatma Gandhi, wrote:

> *Your beliefs become your thoughts*
> *Your thoughts become your words*
> *Your words become your actions*
> *Your actions become your habits*
> *Your habits become your values*
> *Your values become your destiny*

And, as a call from the ancients, the same song of vibration:

> *You are what your deep, driving desire is.*
> *As your desire is, so is your will.*
> *As your will is, so is your deed.*
> *As your deed is, so is your destiny.*
> —*Brihadaranyaka Upanishad IV. 4.5*

One of the breakthroughs in quantum physics is the awareness and acceptance that there is much that we do not know and cannot see with our limited five senses. And so it is with spiritual understanding.

The ultimate experience of truth beyond this world may seemingly be unfathomable or indescribable for many of us. Human language is certainly a limited vehicle of expression for these truths. As spiritual students and teachers (we are always both), however, we can accept these limitations and strive nonetheless to verbalize, live, and express spiritual thoughts and understandings, agreeing to see within, through, and beyond the words shared with one another. We can also choose not to quibble over the names that the general mix of humanity calls the spiritual inner being or *Source* within all of us. Spiritual sages throughout the ages have introduced thousands of names for what many in this world today term as God. We can choose to accept such spiritual references and names as a totality of acceptable and unique language which we can choose to appreciate, tolerate or embrace. I will most often use the terms *God* or *Source* in this writing, taking poetic license to describe that marvelous universal presence in order to more easily facilitate the thought, understandability, and writing process. I have also chosen to use the pronoun *He* in most cases in reference to God rather than to try and juxtapose *she* in companion places. The English language is woefully inadequate when we try to equate gender writing. Writing he/she, or some equivalent verbiage, is cumbersome and awkward. In fact, if not for a linguistic anomaly that there is no neutral pronoun in Hebrew, God could be known in the Western world as *it* rather than *He*. As you read this book please know that the spirit resides in the combination and appreciation of yin and yang, the divine feminine and spirit masculine—both are one—not a separate *He* or *She*.

It is in this spirit that this book is written. Let's proceed together to explore and grow our own spiritual awareness, understanding, and depth by addressing the key questions that are presented in the following chapters...And so it is.

Namaste!
David DiPietro Weiss (2012)

WORKS CITED

1.   A handbook of questions and answers for teaching the tenets of a religion. The Catholics use *The Baltimore Catachism*.
2.   A *Lightseeker* is you—you who have chosen a path to enlightenment. You have opted to enter a path of self realization and have chosen to follow your spiritual journey consisting of love, connection with your source, and a devotion to the soul. A Lightseeker knows that enlightenment is a journey as well as a destination.
3.   See Chapter 14 for a more complete treatise on Quantum Physics.
4.   Gibran, Kahlil, *The Prophet*, pg.55

CHAPTER 1

WHO AM I?

THIS MAY SEEM a strange or redundant question with which to begin. Many of us already think we know who we are. We choose to define ourselves by many monikers. If someone were to ask, "Who are you," how would you answer? I suggest that your first thought would be to share with them your primary career or "role" in this life. One's answer would most likely address one's occupation or social status—such as teacher, lawyer, mother, nurse, carpenter, nobility, millionaire, gardener, truck driver, and so on. All of these and more would seem to suffice as legitimate answers to the question. Most all of us would be satisfied with such an answer and not pursue it further.

But is such an answer adequate? Is such an answer even real? One can suppose it to be adequate if one sees oneself as one who does not presume an afterlife. As a Lightseeker, the question becomes much more esoteric and meaningful when one intuits a life beyond the defined five senses. For example, who are we when we shed this body and transcend to the next plane of existence? As one examines and summarizes the plethora of historical teachings from the myriad of sages and mystics throughout the ages, the evidence seems to weigh heavily on the acceptance of the principle of reincarnation or rebirth. Life goes on, albeit in another realm... and we may be destined to return. Modern Christian theology gives some weight to reincarnation in the sense that it teaches that Jesus resurrected himself. While not technically reincarnation, resurrection presupposes that life has a continuance.[1]

Since the Council of Nicea[2] in 386 A.D., however, Christianity generally has abandoned the theory of individual reincarnation giving credence only to the notable exception of the resurrection of Jesus the Christ. Of course Christian theology also teaches that Jesus, as the Christian Messiah, died for mankind's sins and individuals will ascend by simply accepting Jesus as the savior. Belief in Jesus carries the Christian beyond the realm of samsara or rebirth. In that tradition, reincarnation by modern Catholics is viewed as a moot point.[3]

However, because of the overwhelming postulates throughout recorded history regarding the spiritual logic of reincarnation, this book will base its premise on the *Lightseeker's* acceptance and knowledge of reincarnation.

Yet the questions surrounding reincarnation still baffle our finite minds and conscious spirit. Do we reincarnate in the same form, in the same geographical location, or in the same time period, or even on this singular blue planet in our known solar system? Will we still be a teacher, lawyer, mother, etc? Will we retain our earthly identity in the astral dimensions—that mystical world we enter upon transition from this current life—or will we reappear as another human identity or, perhaps, even embark on a soulful transmigration as another species?

Who Am I? Indeed, a truly deep and intuitive question. Are you a body that has an embedded Soul or are you a Soul who has temporary residence in a body? I use the singular term body because our bodies will change with every new incarnation. Our earthly professions, roles or places in the universe and future existences will change or evolve according to our desires, thoughts and deeds.[4] Pierre Teilhard de Chardin, French philosopher in the 1800s, put it this way:

> *It is misleading to think that you are a physical being having a spiritual experience. Rather take the view that you are a spiritual being having a worldly experience.*

As a young man, the realization that I was a spiritual being temporarily residing in a physical body was a tremendous revelation to me. That single realization transformed my entire understanding of myself and gave me clues as to why I am here.

How we live now will help determine how our next incarnation will unfold. It could be to face new and deeper challenges as we develop our spiritual self. It could also bring forth the same lessons to learn once again in a different form or context, until we understand the depth of our existence and our true relationship with Source. Each time we incarnate is another opportunity for us to repair our separation from Source—from God. The separation from Source keeps us pacing on the great treadmill, the eternal circle of birth and rebirth. It keeps us from returning to our real self, with God.

Our incarnation is divinely designed by Source to fill our every desire, even those desires we only *thought* we desired.

So then, let us answer our original question, "Who am I?"

We can intuitively know that we are a Soul. We also can intuit that we are a Soul that is temporarily housed in a body—a body that we chose before we entered into this incarnation, and a body that reflects our past karmic actions, needs, and desires. These bodies of ours will eventually wither and die, yet the Soul will live on eternally. Let's face it, the old axiom, "You can't take *it* with you," is highly apropos. The *it* we can't take with us includes every tangible thing, every material possession, every passing thought, including the physical body many of us cherish and believe to be *real*.

None of the roles or jobs with which we moniker ourselves will continue intact to the next incarnation. Nor will our personalities necessarily survive—although the essential lessons we have learned in this present incarnation can survive and flourish in the next because of the *Karma* we have seeded in this one.[5] The lessons that we have learned can be accessed in each incarnation, drawing from perhaps hundreds of previous incarnations, by listening and paying attention to your *intuition*.

Intuition is the words and thoughts of your Source communicated to us, through us. It is our so called and much ballyhooed, *sixth sense*. Intuition can be the voice of God speaking to us. It is often said that intuitive prayer is when we talk to God, and meditation is when God talks to us. As *Lightseekers,* we need to talk with God through prayer and truly listen through meditation! Perhaps the true answer to the question *Who am I* may be simply put, *I am a child of God and I am on a journey to oneness with the Source.*

WORKS CITED

1. In general parlance, resurrection connotes a return to the same body while reincarnation refers to returning in a different body.

2. Called by Emperor Constantine in 325 A.D to reconcile the differences in Christianity with over 165 bishops from throughout the empire. It was here that the sanctity of Jesus Christ, deemed both human and spirit, was also affirmed.

   Later, at the Fifth Ecumenical Council at Constantinople in 553 A.D., in the reign of Roman emperor Justinian, all traces of reincarnation were ordered stricken from inclusion in the biblical writings because the originals of many of the Bible's books were loaded with references to reincarnation. Early church leaders found it very difficult to control their flocks without the hell, fire, and brimstone approach that only one life lends itself to…although it was informally still recognized and practiced by many. Only hints of reincarnation appear in the King James version of the Bible (Matthew 17; Matthew 11:14-15; Malachi 4:5.)

3. It is interesting to note that in a PEW poll, (2009) 28-30 percent of Catholics indicate that they believe in reincarnation and 49% of the general population say they believe they had a mystical, religious, or spiritual experience in their lives.

4. A scientific investigation of reincarnation and near death experiences (NDE) is chronicled in a comprehensive study by Jeffrey Long, M.D. in his book *Evidence of the Afterlife*. Additional information on past life experiences are presented by Michael Newton, PhD. in his book *Journey of Souls—Case Studies of Life Between lives*. Newton specializes in past life regressions looking specifically into the "space between lives."

5. Karma is the Hindu term for Cause and Effect. It is described as the principle that makes every man and woman the cause of their present global location, lifestyle, intelligence, relatives and physical body condition.

CHAPTER 2

HOW DID I GET HERE?

E VERY ONE OF us at one time or another in our present
existence has pondered the question of how we got here.
Perhaps early in your life one of the first thoughtful questions you
asked your mom and dad had to do with where you came from.
If your parent followed the usual script, there was either a halting
conversation as they struggled to discuss with you the physical
emergence of your body while skimming over any significant role
of sex, or they avoided the subject as much as possible by suggesting
some preposterous story that emulates or parallels the fairy tale
that the stork brought you.

Perhaps later in life you were sent to a bible study, church,
or synagogue, where you were taught the spiritual beliefs and
practices of your family or peers. There, you didn't have to ask
the question, they simply presented you with answers as best they

knew them as they were taught and thought they knew. Then, each spiritual organization, with its own unique methodology, taught its exclusive and treasured understandings and beliefs about the physical presence of our precious body and why it was important to listen and accept what they wanted you to learn.[1] This, of course, was your introduction to the meaning of life.

Drawing on the experiences of those same mystics and sages referenced earlier, Biblical, Hebrew, and Christian references and interpretations, ancient writings of the Hindu Vedas, The Koran, The Torah and the alchemy of the Kaballa, some important conclusions can be inferred.

First we can postulate that we came from the same place we are going…home—not such a complicated answer when viewed from a *Lightseeker's* perspective. When we are *born* we burst upon the earthly scene through a miraculous process that uses as a vehicle one's mother and father. They, in turn, had merged their physical bodies together to plant the seed of our existence. But, of course, you knew that! This is not to be a course in marriage and family life or, as my parents would call it, a discussion of *"you know what."*

We can begin by remembering what Kahlil Gibran said in his greatest work, *The Prophet*, regarding our children or, indeed, ourselves as children.

> *Your children are not your children. They are the sons and daughters of Life's longing for itself. They come through you, but not from you. And though they are with you, they belong not to you…You may house their bodies, but not their souls.*[2]

And so we may consider our bodies as individual temporary vehicles, just as we can consider our parents as the physical portals that made our *birth* possible and were chosen to care for us while beginning this special journey. Of course, when we continue on the *Lightseeker's* spiritual path, we view life not with a beginning or end, but as a continuum through consciousness from and into another dimension. And, as an aspiring *Lightseeker*, one recognizes that the intrinsic beauty of spirit can come to any individual, at any time in life, any place in the universe, either because of, or in spite of, religious training or upbringing.

We know that death is not the opposite of life. Death is the opposite of birth, and *birth* is the opposite of death. It is all part of the eternal process. Our bodies will wilt, wither, and die as will our brain and all its ego and memory. But our brain and Mind are separate. The Mind, or true consciousness, takes up residence in the brain and when the brain dies, as it will, the Mind continues sans the body. There is no death, except as we perceive it in the time-space continuum we have created. This consciousness is the base of our spiritual connections.

Consciousness, that which presents intuition, insight, imagination and choice, is not considered a product of the brain, but of the Mind. Thoughts are *localized* within the brain and the brain serves as the physical vehicle to allow the body to perform in various scenarios of purpose. There is strong evidence that these thought functions do not emanate from the brain, but from the Mind, or consciousness. They exist *outside* of the space-time continuum—and time doesn't exist in that continuum.[3]

Not so long ago, most of this genre of spiritual thought was considered theoretical and mystical, and consequently dismissed as a fantasy or superstition promulgated by early fringe scientists, alchemists, and sometimes comically perceived mystical wizards. Today science and religion (i.e. spirit) are merging to reflect a common ground in what has been termed as *New Thought*. So many studies by physicists, doctors, biological scientists, coupled with sophisticated brain and biological studies, show more and more evidence that there is more to us than our physical bodies. Science, it seems, especially studies of the brain, cellular biology and quantum physics, have been rapidly merging thought, consciousness, and theory as more modern knowledge is revealed. Some physicists and many spiritual prophets see us actually facing the limits of knowledge and suggest that we are in the twilight of the scientific age and the birth of a new age of consciousness.

Most quantum scientists term this consciousness as *Non-Local*,[4] occurring *outside* the body. This thought opens up and matches the new truth of the quantum world to reveal astonishing non-local abilities to project, travel, and heal as we have never before understood, much less imagined.

So back to our original question, "How did I get here?" The answer is esoteric inasmuch as it seems to be that we have *always* been HERE—except HERE is not the here with which we are familiar on this earthly plane. Life could be termed a timed visit, an interval, or *way station*, on our perpetual journey in consciousness. But knowing that we are primarily a soul having a temporary 3rd dimensional experience, this life is only an illusionary and temporary existence when matched against the true HERE.

WORKS CITED

1. There has always been debate on whether a parent should or should not point their child in the direction of the family religion. Religious training in the family tradition is most often viewed as another rite of passage in growing up, another form of family required schooling. Not providing a formal moral educational and a common religious compass and belief, is a family fear that the child would not have a spiritual base with which to understand his or her precarious place in this world. The competing fear of exposing children to various socially acceptable religious sects because that's what "good people" do, offended some families as a form of indoctrination and desired for the child to experience his or her own spiritual quests and decide when *they* were *ready*. We'll not argue the merits of either side.

2. Gibran, *The Prophet*, "On children," pg. 17.

3. Time itself is shown to be a temporary state according to Quantum Physics. It, therefore, is considered to be an illusion. And, as we begin understanding quantum theory and the teachings of ancient spiritual sages, so is our physical existence.

4. Refers to projecting beyond the human body by entering the quantum field allowing humans in physical form to act in another dimension through one's Mind or consciousness.

CHAPTER 3

HOW CAN I KNOW MY PURPOSE?

THIS, PERHAPS, IS the most intriguing question man has pondered since the beginning of his existence on this planet. Initially early man was simply concerned about survival. As he evolved and his basic needs became generally satisfied, his mind began to probe the seeming magic of his existence and he began to question. Why are we here? Are we here to play? Are we here to have a good time? And are we here to enjoy the physical beauty and pleasures that the planet earth provides? Or, conversely, are we here to suffer the pain, loneliness, poverty, sickness and tragedies that we witness collectively each day? Are we here to do both, alternating days of pleasure and suffering that dot each of our lives, some experiencing more the pleasure, others noting an abundance of suffering? Why's that?

This is truly a magnificent question and suggests an elegant answer. As we think about and examine the array of basic emotions that we experience daily, emotions such as despair, anger, joy, contentment, frustration, empowerment, disempowerment, as well as many others, we find ourselves experiencing these emotions as they are captured in the five sensory recesses of our mind, and those sensual emotions dominate our thoughts. If we sift through and categorize these emotions, we find that they naturally separate into two camps. There are only two emotions in this universe. One is Fear, the other is Love. However, only Love is real. Fear is a conjure of our corporeal existence. We create it. It truly doesn't exist except as a manifestation in our minds. In retrospect, we can't think of Love as the opposite of Fear. Love can not have an opposite because it is all encircling, all encompassing, and can have no opposing counterpoint.

Regularly, my life can produce emotions that only I can attempt to control. When I feel the onset of grief, despair, anger or other negative emotions, I must trust myself to choose the next highest thought. That thought might be acceptance or frustration, both of which are a higher vibration than grief or other "lower" emotions. However, I am constantly choosing my thoughts to escape from whatever negative emotion that I am feeling. Otherwise, I unwittingly choose to wallow in my grief and turmoil, a fearful existence. All these negative thoughts I mention above get their power from fear. However, I find that I have the unique power to change my thoughts, as do you, to thoughts of Love, Joy and Empowerment. I can't change "what is" but I *can* change my attitude and my vibrations towards "what is" and move my emotions towards Love, Joy and Empowerment. That is entirely within my control.

The path of an aspiring *Lightseeker* indicates that the Mind function is to experience *Love,* or *joy* and *empowerment.* Without this Love, we have little or no operating wisdom for we are battling for survival. Without Love and Wisdom, we might appear to be very functional in this world but, in truth, we are lost and treading aimlessly on the great wheel of birth and rebirth continuing a life cycle that brings us back, without substantial spiritual progress, to a human birth time after time.

Some may reason that such a fate is not so bad. Experiencing the accumulation of much wealth and status in this world, those that have it are enjoying it immensely, and this existence may seem more than adequate. But it seems adequate only because they have forgotten who the true self is and that the life of bliss is our true nature devoid of any pain and suffering, replete with total freedom. A contemporary sage opined,

> *The objects of pleasure do not give us happiness. The objects are merely keys to happiness. They momentarily unlock the happiness that is always inside us.[1]*

In general, we do not remember true bliss. We live in an illusion, a *temporary* world that will inexorably wither and die. We don't realize this of course, because we are too preoccupied with the distractions of everyday life in an attempt to satisfy whatever our egos seem to require. It's difficult for many to understand that what we are experiencing in this external, physical world is an illusion because it seems so *real,* doesn't it? What a bizarre concept to think that what we have come to know and believe as reality, is to be an illusion. How do we reconcile that to our human experience which tends to reject such thinking?

The esteemed Greek philosopher Plato, attempted to explain this illusionary concept in his classic essay, *The Allegory of the Cave*, from his most recognized work, *The Republic*. Plato described symbolically the predicament in which mankind finds itself. He opined his belief that the world revealed by our five senses is not the real world. That what we see, touch, hear, smell, and taste is an illusion and, indeed, a poor facsimile of what is real.

In his allegory he envisions man living in an underground cave. The cave's mouth has an opening from which a blinding light projects all along the cave and forward against a reflective wall in front of mankind. All the inhabitants of the cave, however, are mentally chained so they cannot move and can only see what's in front of them, the walls of the cave. The mental chains prevent them from turning their heads back towards the bright and blinding light. Behind them is a bright fire blazing and casting a shadow of their figures on the cave wall in front of them.

Mankind thus sees only their own reflections cast upon the wall in front of them projected by the light behind them—much like seeing screen actors playing a role in a movie. What they observe is mankind passing across the screen going through life in a world that is actually their own shadows—illusions of themselves—projected by the blinding light behind them. Mankind only is able to see such shadows as they never move their heads which are transfixed upon the screen.

Plato postulates that if the cave's echo and light come from behind, the source of light and sound, mankind would surely not pause to look around, but would assume that such energy would actually come from the shadows appearing on the screen. All they choose to hear and see would be the shadows on the wall while ignoring the light behind. The reflections, echoes, and light from behind are seemingly emanating from the cave wall in front of them on which their attention is focused.

Plato goes on to say that if released from the mental chains and made aware of the light from behind them, mankind could stand up and think to walk towards the light, rather than continue to believe the shadows projected on the wall. However, in doing so, they would suffer distressingly sharp pains from the bright glare of the light and would be unable to see or be comfortable with the new and true realities of the light. This distressing pain could easily prompt them to turn their heads back around to the cave wall where their own images were projected, even though knowing that those images, so long observed and believed, were only shadows. And even as they recognize that the images they saw and historically believed earlier were illusions, they will still turn their heads back to the comfortable and familiar illusory cave wall projections.

However, by having the courage to turn their heads and look into the light, mankind has the opportunity to approach and initiate an understanding of the true reality. Their eyes can reveal their true origins and existence while staring into the light. By becoming accustomed to the initial light blinding, they now have the opportunity for a clear vision.

"What will be man's reply," Plato asks, "Will he not be perplexed? Will man not prefer the comfortable shadows on the wall even as he is shown the fallacy of his beliefs and is introduced to the light, the truth?" If compelled to look straight into the light, will he not suffer such pain in his eyes that turning away and returning to those painless shadow objects will be more compelling—even more compelling then the truth now revealed to him?

Hmm. Quite a dilemma Plato poses. To him, mankind is more comfortable in the shadow world, the world of illusion.

It takes a leap of faith to justify an entirely new notion that the world around us is an illusion. It certainly does represent a blinding light and challenges us to rethink what we think we know.

Plato's faith, however, tells him that the universe ultimately is good and spiritually enlightened individuals and teachers will appear when called and needed. He suggests that those called beings have an obligation to society to use their wisdom to help the masses on the road to enlightenment. Plato never suggested that he was one of those called teachers, even as he penned his theories.

The 20th century mystic and teacher from India, Paramahansa Yogananda (1893–1952), put it this way:

> *Man has falsely identified himself with the pseudo-soul or ego. When he transfers his sense of identity to his true being, his immortal Soul, he discovers that all pain is unreal. He no longer can even imagine the state of suffering.*[2]

So then, life is an illusion! Wow, what a difficult concept to wrap ourselves around! Let's examine this conundrum.

Each moment we are bombarded by a myriad of thoughts that race through and across our minds. Our thoughts create images of all that we seem to visualize through our five senses. As we see and think and synthesize our continuous pattern of thought, our brain forms images of what we experience with those comfortable and familiar five senses. Those images become embedded in our brains and become and sustain our so-called *reality*. Because we live in a finite world, a world trapped in time, complete with beginnings and endings, we process those images and create our own stage, characters, our own projection system and movie screen—indeed, our own cave wall.

In a sense, we are rambling and jousting with fear, following the instincts of our egos, instead of embracing Love. Holding off fear and trying to recognize and avoid fear pervades our daily lives.

Let us remind ourselves that when we speak of Love in a spiritual context, it is not the common characterization that we usually emote around. Love isn't some material object or an emotion attached to a supposed "loved one." We have spent our lives identifying, assuming, and accepting this as Love's sole definition. Yes, physical and emotional love is evident in the outer physical world but, in truth, it is a reflection of the cosmic Spiritual Love. It is a gift of the infinite world.

Spiritual Love is an ethereal expression of God, uniquely manifested in positive emotions and acts such as joy, kindness, compassion, forgiveness, peace, non-judgment, mercy, intimacy and other companion thoughts. When you live with love in your heart, you live in *Heaven* on Earth.

When you have fear in your heart and exhibit the negative emotions of anger, selfishness, judgment, obsession, war, and violence plus a myriad of other negative thoughts, you exist in *Hell* on Earth. When we share those negative thoughts and actions in the physical world, we project ourselves into a living Hell. That would explain the suffering, both individual and collectively, in which we all participate as a group. We form our own collective Hell by living with too much fear and too little Love. Our negative thoughts attract companion negative thoughts and propel our negative outlook on life.

Being with your Source, being with God, means to think with Love. We are who we *think* we are. We all have a positive purpose while living on this planet.

Marianne Williamson, noted author and spiritual teacher said this:

> *We are all assigned a piece of the "Garden," a corner of the universe that is ours to transform. Our corner of the universe is our own life—our relationships, our homes, our work—our current circumstances exactly as they are. Every situation we find ourselves in is an opportunity, perfectly planned by Devine Spirit, to teach love instead of fear.*[3]

That is our purpose. We can choose to tend our "garden" with love and reap the benefits here on earth and for ourselves and our next incarnation, or we can choose to live in our fear induced hell. Source provides one's every desire.

Your thoughts and actions in this plane, mitigated and influenced by your unique karma, determine how your life plays out. There is no escape from the law of Karma. You "reap what you sow" is a common idiom as is "Do unto others as you would do unto yourself," the so called "golden rule." The ancient *Code of Hammurabi* produced "an eye for an eye and a tooth for a tooth," a rather primitive law of man's retribution that reflect a tenet of the law of Karma. However, it is your choice how you live. *It is always your choice.*

And what does following the Word of God get you, one might ask expectantly? One looks around and sees fearful people with strong egos "succeeding" in this world. They seem to have everything; money, power, fame, luck. "I think I am a good person," we say to ourselves, "I follow God with joy and love. Why am I not lucky and successful?"

We must be wary of what we construe as good news or bad news. How many of us have experienced what we deduced was misfortune only to later recognize a new vista of opportunity that we didn't see coming? We have all heard the axiom, "When a door closes, a window opens." This axiom has rung true so many times in my life that I can't recount them all. What might have appeared to me as bad news when I lost my job became a blessing when I was guided towards a much more spiritually rewarding career and opportunity. I can easily assume that the same has happened to you or a loved one on many occasions.

Thinking of good or bad news, I am reminded of the ancient Buddhist story about a farmer who was considered to be a fortunate rich man because he had a horse with which to plow his field. The neighbors envied this man while acknowledging that he was kind, considerate and worked hard despite being the only person in the area who had a working horse.

One day the horse ran away. The neighbors came to consol him.

"That's too bad," they said, "That is very unlucky!"

"Perhaps," quietly replied the farmer.

A week later the horse returned and brought back with it five healthy stray horses.

The neighbors were astonished and pleased for the farmer.

"You are so very lucky," said the neighbors. "We are pleased at the turn of your fortune."

"Perhaps," quietly replied the farmer.

A couple of days later the farmer's only son was breaking in the new horses when he was thrown from the back of one of the animals and broke both his legs, leaving the farmer to work the farm by himself.

"We are so sorry," said the neighbors. "That is such bad news and such a terrible burden to have placed on you and your son."

"Perhaps," quietly replied the farmer.

And so while the farmer struggled to work his farm alone while his son healed, the military came into the village to conscript all the young men to fight in the Great War. They passed over the farmer's son because of his disability. Many of the young villagers who went to war did not come back.

A simple story that well illustrates the axiom that bad fortune or good luck can be fleeting. One cannot know whether it is "good luck" or "bad luck" that we experience. We cannot know the future but can acknowledge that bad luck may well be a hidden blessing trapped in illusionary events wrapped in meaningless time.

The farmer knew that... So should we.

When we encounter adversity we can ask ourselves, tell ourselves, that there is a lesson here and in it can be a blessing, if we're strong enough to accept it. This moment, in the NOW, is exactly what it is. It simply *is*. When you struggle with *what is* in the moment, you are struggling with the universe. It is important to understand that when you accept the moment, you accept things as they are rather than what you wished them to be. I am not inferring that these moments can not be incredibly painful or seemingly just or unjust—they just *are*. Your *acceptance* frees you from *attachment* to the pain and eventually will free you from the pain. You will soon look back and realize that it was all an illusion, not real, because you are in a new NOW.

The miracle of acceptance is much like turning your boat downstream after struggling upstream against the currents and, instead, deciding to go with the flow. When you accept *what is,* you release your fear and anxiety and live the axiom taught to us by a familiar song.

"Row, row, row your boat, gently down the stream, merrily, merrily, merrily, merrily—*life is but a dream.*" Downstream is your true divine path and acceptance is one of your spiritual directives. Remember, a miracle is simply a change in perception, an ode to Love, and miracles are always within your power. With a change in perception, and with the dominion of Love, you should *expect* miracles.

And so I conclude this chapter with how I started it. The question was; "What is my purpose in Life? The answer is: "My purpose is to LOVE." When we direct our thoughts to that universal love and acceptance, fear reveals itself as merely an illusion.

WORKS CITED

1.   Deshapriya.

2.   Paramahansa Yogananda, *Where There Is Light*, pg. 20

3.   Williamson, Marianne, *A Return To Love,* pg. 66

CHAPTER 4

WHO OR WHAT IS GOD?

W HAT A QUESTION! But what an intriguing and important question! First, we must establish whether there is a God, and in an authentic and understanding way, before we can begin our quest to find him.

There has been much written to prove or disprove the existence of God, but it seems that the greatest proof comes from within and has not been examined or realized by most of us. It is fascinating, however, to examine the background of human historical *proofs* of God in order to understand the thinking of humankind. In our finite world we have struggled to define and understand the omnipotent and infinite figure we postulate to be God.

Several of the classic proofs of God come from the writings of St. Thomas Aquinas, an early theologian who—along with St. Augustine—formed the early Christian proofs related to God's existence. It is Aquinas' work that has defined, up until recently, our collective beliefs about the question of whether God exists.

In his work, *Summa Theologica,* he proposes the following proofs.

1) *Movements:* Aquinas, initially, suggests that in the universe everything is in motion. Indeed, if everything is in motion, it has to be moved. If everything is moving, then something moved everything. He goes on to suggest that this cannot regress in an infinite motion but must have a Prime Mover. He says, "Therefore it is necessary to arrive at a first mover, moved by no other; and this everyone understands to be God."

Hmmm, if we espouse this theory then perhaps we might ask the question if God himself would need to be moved.

2) *Cause & Effect:* The universe is a series of causes and effects is another postulate by Aquinas. Every cause has an effect and every effect has a cause. Therefore there must be a *first cause.*

Sounds very logical, doesn't it? If the universe exists, there must have been a cause—some force that was needed to initiate the first cause.

Many modern folks, however, ascribe to what is now called the "Big Bang" theory—that which is scientifically and theoretically presented by physicist Stephen Hawkings, among many other esteemed thinkers.

Aquinas said, "Therefore it is necessary to admit a first efficient cause, to which everyone gives the name of God." Well, this reads much like the first proof, doesn't it? Who or what caused God might be the next question.

3) *Possibilities*: In this next *proof,* Aquinas seems to touch inadvertently on quantum mechanics when discussing his theory of *possibilities*. To Aquinas, possibilities are just that—possible. If everything is a possibility, then conversely, there could indeed be, theoretically, *no* possibilities. But if there were no possibilities then there would be nothing—no existence at all. The universe exists. Aquinas suggests, "therefore we must admit the existence of some being having of itself its own necessity, and not receiving it from another, but rather causing in others this necessity. This all men speak of as God."

4) *Goodness*: Another Aquinas *proof* of God suggests that goodness, truism, best, and nobility are the root of God. All these terms intensify on a gradual scale of good. Aquinas theorizes that "There is then, something which is truest, something best—something noblest. Therefore there must be something which is to all beings the cause of their being, goodness, and every other perfection. And this we call God." There can be nothing greater that can be conceived.

5) *Clockwork*: The last *proof* suggested by Aquinas approaches a more modern interpretation based on his examination of how the universe is designed. Its intricate design, which reflects perfection, sophistication and the evolution of life, suggests a clockwork movement rather than a chaotic randomness. Aquinas says that "natural bodies act for an end...therefore some intelligent beings exist by whom all natural things are ordered to their end; and this being we call God."

As we can see, it has been impossible to *logically* and *empirically* prove the existence of God. And, as Aquinas attempts to account for the existence of God, each of his suggestions is a postulate founded in logic with a qualitative leap into a spiritual consideration. However, it seems that it is much easier to prove that God *doesn't* exist if we follow logic and finite thinking. Each of the proofs cannot be proved valid by logic. All proofs eventually demand faith as the motivating and accepting precept. Most of our *proofs* have been based on assumption and those assumptions are based on our historical patterns of thinking. And, because humans are pattern-seeking beings, all these proofs fall into an "illogical-logical" pattern, and we historically have chosen to accept them. We assume, therefore, because of our historical pattern-seeking, there must have been a first cause, a prime mover, a clockwork of design by a designer or other like postulates because that's all we seem to know, or care to know. All of the above proofs assume a concept of time, and time is a finitely created illusion. But then we've already indicated elsewhere that time itself is an illusion. Is this a circular argument? It certainly seems so. If so, how do we prove to ourselves that God truly exists? Who or what then, is God?

The answer is incredibly simple, once you understand the purpose of why you exist.

You are God! (Gasp!)

And I am also. And everyone and everything we see in our sensual world is God. And we know it—intuitively! God speaks to us every day. He speaks to all his children. We are all God, or more precisely, we are all part of God, as God is part of us. That includes the entire universe, together with rocks, water, animals and plants. We are *all* part of God. We are all one!

How do we prove it?

We don't have to. At least not in a logical sense. Yet, science is opening the gate for a merger with spirituality. This is not simply finite science, this is infinite Spirit. God is continually proving himself and we, and science, are waking up to his lessons. Just look at the relatively new discovery of quantum mechanics. The basic laws of physics advanced by Sir Isaac Newton in the 1600s captured and have until recently held hostage our belief systems of cause and effect for hundreds of years. The laws of Newtonian physics are taught in every major school and university in the world and we have accepted those laws in theory and fact because we see demonstrations of those laws in our everyday five-sensory world. And they are a foundation for understanding, not necessarily wrong, just incredibly incomplete.

Newtonian physics seems to work well in our macro world, where we have crude measuring devices to record movement based on measurable constants. But, it loses much of its usefulness when applied to the subatomic world, including the cellular biological world. Newtonian physics do not apply to that world to the astonishment and surprise to all of us, including learned physicists such as Albert Einstein.

Now, enter *quantum physics* [1] and our whole world is turned upside down and inside out. Quantum physics has proved at the sub-atomic level that thought—yes, thought—thinking, can change what is.

In other words, what you think can allow *you* to create a new reality and a new perspective. By quantum experiences and experiments, quantum physics is proving to us that our powers are much more than we suppose them to be, and we are not simply residents of a limited sensory world. There are many solid examples that have demonstrated this, especially the work of classic physicists such as Einstein, Max Planck, Niels Bohr, Eric Schrodinger, Werner Heisenberg, Max Born, James Frank, Gustav Hertz and others.

More recently the work of cellular biologist, Dr. Bruce Lipton, *(Power of the Cells)* shows us that we are able to change and influence the working of our own cellular structure, our individual cells, through *thought*...a discovery promulgated through Dr. Lipton's understanding of quantum physics.[2] Lipton brings to biological life the axiom many have repeated, "Change your thoughts, change your life."

So what!, you might say.

Well, here's what.

When we understand that material *forces* and material *causes* do not completely determine the future, and that *consciousness* brings forth actuality from possibility, then we know that there is room *for choice*, *(free will), for creativity, and for divine purposes.*

This is, to put it mildly, a *profound change* in our understanding of our perceptions and power. And our power to create is derived from the singular power of creation. We are all one. We are all made up of the same sub-atomic stuff known as atoms, space and molecules. And, as we learn to create, we learn about God. As we learn about God, the more we realize that he is within us and not some mystical bearded fellow sitting on a throne dispensing karmic reward and punishment from on high. Quantum physics has opened up new doors of understanding and has shown us that the essence of possibility and co-creation is always, and always has been, within us and within our grasp. It has been instrumental in closing the once seemingly insurmountable gap between science and spirit, between philosophy and religion. The great thinkers and physicists mentioned earlier, as well as many others have paved the way. They each experienced the fear and difficulty in changing entire thought processes that have been held for centuries. In fact, Eric Schrodinger, a co-discoverer of the new quantum mechanics, when confronted by the facts of his own discovery, stated that if he had known that these quantum leaps were here to stay, he would never have discovered quantum physics![3]

But Einstein said,

The important thing is not to stop questioning. Curiosity has its own reason for existing. One cannot help but be in awe when we contemplate the mysteries of eternity, of life, of the marvelous structure of reality. It is enough if we try merely to comprehend a little of this mystery every day. Never lose a holy curiosity.

Sir James Jeans, a noted English astronomer, said "The world looks more and more like a giant thought than a giant machine."[4]

Once we accept that we are part of God and God is part of us, we only have to learn to practice communicating with our multiple-self entities to make the changes we desire. Let's talk about why we already know how.

Many of us are reflecting upon that power and beginning our learning quest. We now need to practice what we know.

That practice revolves around the two spiritual principles that have graced us since the essential beginning of mankind, *meditation* and *prayer*. It is with these accessible, ancient, sacred, and reliable tools that we are able to communicate with God and him with us. But make no mistake; "*He*" and "*Us*" are the same entity.

There are but two simple understandings to embrace regarding meditation and prayer before we explore more about each in following chapters.

1) Prayer is when we talk to God.

2) Meditation is when God can talk to us.

Meditation is stilling your conscious thoughts long enough to hear and see God within. It is when your mind is still, without conscious thought clogging up the lines of communication, that you hear and see God. It is when you choose to live in the NOW, the only real moment that exists, that you are able to truly realize God.

Remember, there is no past, it is gone forever and there is not a future as it has yet to happen. It is only our ego that continually tugs at us to recreate the past or dream of the future. In recreating such a scenario, the ego can lead us on a fruitless journey. We *can* choose differently.

There is only the NOW. To create your future one does it in the infinite space, and the only moment where we can know infinity is the NOW. Therefore, to let your ego know that God exists, and knowing that your ego often rejects that notion, you simply do both—pray and meditate. Then when you know the power of your consciousness, you will understand and realize a truth that we've ignored for many lifetimes.

So, again the question, "Who is God?"

You are God; God is Love. You are Love. It's really quite simple, isn't it?

WORKS CITED

1. For a wonderful and entertaining understanding of the workings of quantum physics, consult Dr. Fred Alan Wolf's CD Series, *Dr. Quantum, A Users Guide to Your Universe*. Also visit the writings of Amit Goswami, Ph.D. in *The Visionary Window, A Quantum Physicist's Guide to Enlightenment*... and, of course, look over chapter 14 in this book.

2. Lipton, Bruce, Ph.D. *The Biology of Belief: Unleashing the Power of Consciousness, Matter and Miracles*.

3. Heisenberg is considered to be the other founder even as Max Planck discovered the idea of the quantum in the late 1800s.

4. Sir James Jeans: 1877–1946, English physicist and mathematician who was the first to propose that matter is continuously created throughout the universe. Best know as a writer of popular books on astronomy.

CHAPTER 5

TEACHERS, GURUS & GUIDES?

D O YOU REMEMBER a favorite teacher? We all have had someone or have recognized individuals or groups in our lives that either consciously, or by demonstration, taught us some of our most valuable lessons; lessons we have internalized and carry with us today. It could have been a colleague from our school days or perhaps a friend, neighbor or even a member of your own family. That teacher could have simply given you some valuable advice, or perhaps, demonstrated to you an understanding that served a particular moment or taught you a lesson that has resonated throughout your lifetime. You may have learned the lesson immediately, or possibly it became more meaningful when triggered by an event later in your life. Nevertheless, the teacher gave you an understanding, either directly or unwittingly, of something you had never or perhaps only vaguely considered before. When you finally assimilated it into your daily routine and values, it became part of who you are.

Many of us, when we are seeking answers in virtually any arena of our lives, instinctively look for a teacher—someone who purportedly knows or can teach or demonstrate to us the knowledge or qualities we are seeking and has the capacity to assist in helping us making decisions enabling us to become more aware and knowledgeable.

Such are the teachings of current and historical sages, gurus, spiritual teachers, priests and ministers.

Often, when puzzled about the mysteries of life and death, individuals turn to their religious upbringing or spiritual guides to assist in resolving our questions. In many highly organized religious practices, religions depend on the religious organization to do the *legwork* of spiritual questioning, while we, sometimes lazily or without inquiry, choose to accept or reject their conclusions as right or wrong for us. Organized religious tenets can become guides and teachers and followers tend to embrace their guidance, often without question.

Resorting to an acceptance of *blind faith*, we tend to believe and accept a life with few daily spiritual distractions or responsibilities, the bastions of such faith. I sometimes refer to it as a pre-packaged theology, for those who don't choose to take the time to explore intuitive knowledge and/or, engage in experimental faith. A foray into experimental faith or giving credence to one's intuition would, at the very least, open questions for examination without the rote routine of committing to a lemming-like blind faith. But, as I said in my opening chapter—*They get to do that!* All of us are the captains of our own spiritual ship. Each of our teachers can always be available to us and those teachers evoke a chord of resonance depending on whether or not their message connects with us individually and intuitively. More often than not, we grew up in a family or social group that had already accepted the precepts and teachings of a religion's spiritual interpretation and we accepted those teachings that our family group followed.

As we age and/or mature, (and there *is* a difference) we tend to become more independent and selective about whom our teachers should be and often either abandon our family religion(s) and/ or drift into non-spirituality. Such is the result of not taking the opportunity to choose. We may also begin to search anew for our purpose in life.

In the 1960's, a youthful America began a new quest for spirituality that did not necessarily include joining established major religions. Millions of young people rejected, or were confused by historical and common values taught by those religions in order to seek a new spiritual understanding. Many thought they found hints of such spirituality in the experiences brought about by mind-expanding drugs while others began looking Eastward to spiritual practices in Asia and the Indian sub-continent. Others did both. As a result of this spiritual migration, thousands began seeking spiritual teachers from India and Asia. Teachers from these regions also began to visit the USA and offered teaching here. For the Americas, a new era of spirituality seeking had begun.

Perhaps it was the English rock group *The Beatles* who first drew major attention to this phenomenon when they visited, with millions of fans following their every move, the Maharishi Mahesh Yogi, a spiritual teacher who taught them the practice and value of meditation and individual peace and harmony. He was preceded, of course, by others such as Paramahansa Yogananda who swept the spiritual seeking country with his book, *The Autobiography of a Yogi*. Since then the movement has proliferated and many pilgrimages to India and visits by various Gurus from the Asian subcontinent have dominated our times.

From that time on the act of having a spiritual guide has almost become a staple of Western pop culture. Of course, established religions have always indicated that we should follow a guide and they point to particular historical teachers, such as Jesus, Moses, or Mohammed and their writings as prescriptions to follow. Such profound teachers as these are great inspirations and proponents of love, gratitude and forgiveness.

Eastern spirituality was championed by such teachers as Chinese master *Lao Tzu*—reputedly the author of the *Tao de Ching*; *Siddartha Gautama,* (Known as the Buddha*); Confucious; Kirpal Singh*; *Swami Vivekanananda; Chuang-Tse,* and others who preached that the road to enlightenment is reached through meditation, forgiveness, gratitude, and acceptance of what is.

Many spiritual teachers regard the concept of *angels* with extreme reverence, each teacher giving angels names that befit their culture and time. Accordingly, many folks look to angels as their guides. We have all heard the concept of a guardian angel and many times we say to ourselves, "I think I was just led or protected by my Guardian Angel," without paying any mind to the efficacy of such a statement. Guardian Angels have always been part of our spiritual understanding. Over the centuries many manuscripts have been written about angels, hierarchies compiled, and wisdom translated from earlier spiritual manuscripts depicting and teaching angelic inspired paths to enlightenment. Much of the angel lore was written by early sages, mystics and prophets. In early Christianity, angelic lore carried the same weight as the biblical books, but slipped into history when left out of the Old Testament. Angels such as Gabriel and Michael are both mentioned in the Old Testament. Raphael, the Angel of Healing, appears in the Orthodox Bible but not in the Hebrew Bible. Angels are often described as the *Men in White* because they were seen as male genders clothed in white linen even as most spiritual writings do not declare angels to have a gender.

Western culture and the religions of Abraham—Christianity, Judaism and Islam—all cite angels in their prophesies. For example, it was the angel Gabriel that spoke directly to Mohammed and dictated to him, over a 23 year span, the holy book of Islam, *The Koran*. One can see that the influence of angels has formed the foundation of many spiritual and religious schools of thought.

Spirituality welcomes as guides a wide assortment of angels, deities, saints, ascended masters, gods and goddesses. There are a number of teachers that one can select for one's spiritual journey. These teachers exist and appear in all parts of the world. In many South American countries they appear as spiritual *Shamans*. Native Americans have their medicine man or holy man, also monikered Shamans, who communicate with the spirits for healing and sustenance. Each teacher provides teachings on how to live one's life so one may understand and accept the whys and wherefores of this existence while preparing disciples for the transition to the next life.

Virtually all spirit guides teach, in one form another, a version of the golden rule—*Do unto others as you would have others do unto you*. Most guides also teach forgiveness—forgiveness for oneself and forgiveness for others. Forgiveness must be a daily, moment by moment, practice that requires timeless diligence.

It is often difficult, in a world of cynics, to think of spiritual teachers as wise sages when they appear in modern times. There are, however, many present, available, and offering their wisdom throughout the world. Some are highly publicized and revered for their remarkable skills at interpreting and making understandable the teachings and scriptures of past masters. Individuals active in our Western culture such as Deepak Chopra, Wayne Dyer, Marianne Williamson, Ken Wilber, Jerry and Esther Hicks (Abraham), Eckhart Tolle, Jack Kornfield, Andrew Harvey, and Patricia Cota-Robles are representative of the modern teachers who have dedicated their lives to bringing spiritual awareness to the masses. *(There are many others and I mention several of them in a bibliographical list of references at the end of this book.)* Their writings and seminars are so much more available to us now then access to the ancient sages because of the mass universal communication marvels we have in present times.

Channeled writings such as *A Course in Miracles* have offered profound teachings based on love and forgiveness. A *Course in Miracles* has guided many to right action and profound guidance. I recommend it highly for all *Lightseekers.*

One may choose to incorporate as teachers, ancient writings such as those appearing in the Hindu scriptures of the *Upanishads* or the basic teachings of the Hindus in the historical *Vedas - Rig, Yajur or Saam,* the birthplace of ancient spiritual thought. One cannot dismiss the *Bhagavad Gita* (Song of the Lord) with its rich dialog between *Lord Sri Krishna* and the mighty Pandava warrior, *Arjuna.*[1] These dialogues on the path to enlightenment are required reading for millions of Hindus.

Other teachers, usually as mediums, channel entities from the past, invoke the wisdom of the ages through their teachings. There are countless mediums that channel various sages residing in the nether world, bringing their teachings to this world by yet another means.

Generally speaking, one is able to recognize a true spiritual teacher through intuition and practice. By the law of attraction and one's continually expanding experiences and ritual practice of spirituality, the right spiritual teacher is destined to appear to you.

The search for truth remains our individual quest and responsibility. Basic truth tests we can utilize to determine a true spiritual teacher, are founded on two simple premises as follows. Access to God doesn't demand your money; and your selected guide, teacher, or guru must answer *all* questions you pose—and answer them to your complete understanding and satisfaction.

So who is your teacher? Do you have one? Have you had many and embrace that what makes sense to you from each? Is your teacher a friend whose life you surmise is on a path that you admire? Are you your own teacher as suggested by Andrew Harvey in his book, *The Direct Path*? Are you ready to search for a teacher and follow him or her as you seek your spiritual path? Don't be shy in this search as you are invited to begin with *experimental faith*, not blind acceptance. Such faith is part of your spiritual heritage and allows you to look inside and test the teacher, while assimilating those practices and beliefs that respond to your positive intuition.

WORKS CITED

1. In the Bhagavad Gita (9.17), the Avatar Krishna says to Arjuna, the warrior, "I am the father of this universe, the mother, the support and the grandsire. I am the object of knowledge, the purifier and the syllable Om'. I am also the Rig, Sama and the Yajur Vedas."

CHAPTER 6

WHAT IS PRAYER?

What is the point of prayer? Are prayers really heard and,
if so, by whom or what? What form should prayer take?

PERHAPS YOU HAVE asked yourself these questions over and over or, conversely, simply recited a prayer by mouthing the words either aloud or to oneself without thinking about the sacred meaning or instruction. An overwhelming number of us have learned the Lord's Prayer and have heard and recited it many times. Do we sincerely listen to our prayers or do we simply respond in rote, out of habit, circumstance, or tradition?

Many spiritual traditions use beads to assist disciples in repeating prayers. For example, the Catholic Rosary is a series of beads that remind us to alternate between the Hail Mary and Lord's Prayer with an act of contrition or the creed of the apostles.

The Vedic beads, numbering 108 mantra repetitions, are spiritual reminders of prayer. One has to be sincere in the repetitive prayer ritual so as to concentrate on the meaning and feelings of the prayer. A sure tell-tale sign of non-sincerity are the figurative *rope burns* on one's fingers after rushing through the beads. One might equate the act of rushing through a prayer or prayer beads as similar to running through a museum. Both acts should take time and commitment to be meaningful and effective. So let's examine our motivations and what prayer is and how best to embrace it.

Prayer is our way of talking to God. It's not, obviously, really a conversational dialogue with God, but a sincere and often pleading individual monologue. It is here where we ask God for help, for healing, for assistance with anything that disturbs us so we can alleviate the pain, suffering or trauma, no matter for whom or for what purpose the prayer is intended to address. Kirpal Singh, Indian Guru and a spiritual guide of the 20th century, said this.

Prayer has been defined as an anguished cry of the soul in distress or helplessness, to a Power fuller and greater than itself, for relief and comfort. It is considered an invocation to God, a source competent enough to grant solace and peace to a mind tortured by the problems of life and life's surroundings.[1]

Such a definition can be shifted and interpreted differently according to those who choose to do so, but it brings a universal and common message. The question we could ask next is "What should a prayer be about?" There is a simple answer that resonates throughout the ages. A true prayer is one of *gratitude*. Gratitude is having the vision and grace to accept what is and counting our blessings for what we have. This is an effective prayer that should always be practiced. Does that mean we shouldn't ask for something for ourselves or others; for example, a healing or an intervention to what seems potentially threatening? The answer is, of course you should. However, the main attribute for effective prayer is that you have already recognized that what is, *is*. The act for which you pray for is already proceeding by divine guidance, although it may not necessarily be in the direction that you personally wish to experience. It is your job to align your particular vibration with that for which you pray. That will depend on your ability to accept *what is* and face *what is* with joy. It is in this state of acceptance that your prayer is received and acted upon.

In prayer, after thoughts of gratitude, we may make suggestions or express preferences. We acknowledge that whatever, whoever, we are wishing intercession for is going to be brought about by our own belief; or, in the case of others for whom we pray, by the activation of their own faith. Others have the power to change their *reality* as surely as do you. Your prayers have the effect of affirming your preferences with your Source, as well as affirming the quantum power within you to co-create with God, and creating a shift in your perception. Any shift in *perception* is a miracle and an answer to a prayer. That shift in perception becomes the new truth and obviates any sickness or malady you had previously perceived. This is what is attainable in a prayer. Instead of saying as a prayer, *"Please, dear God, heal this illness,"* consider that the prayer should invoke the power of God within you to change your thoughts and to accept the consequences of what is. At the same moment that you are co-creating the healing truth of the new fact that you are already healed, you are closing the vibrational gap between what is and that for which you pray. Your perfect self is always healed because it was never ill. An illness is part of the illusion.

For example, a prayer could be constructed this way:

Thank you God, for all the blessings you have bestowed upon me. I acknowledge that I am your child and I know your divine plan for me is righteous. My prayer is to affirm that I would prefer to have this malady healed and although I don't fully understand your plan, I pray for your divine guidance to help me understand and accept what is and accede to your gracious will. Thank you God, ...and so it is.

A prayer may also be invoked to ask for sustenance to continue one's devotional practices, such as meditation and selfless service. Such a prayer simply affirms the need to have the strength to do the work of seeking God. Most spirit masters teach their disciples to pray for their needs, as would appear from the following excerpt of a prayer from Kabir, a notable and memorable Sikh mystic.

One cannot meditate with hunger gnawing within,
Take thou the rosary away from me, O Lord.
Grant unto me flour, ghee and salt besides some pulse,
That I may have a day's ration to live upon.
A cot, a pillow with a bed and a quilt,
That I may meditate on Thee undisturbed.
I have not been greedy in my demands,
For I love nothing better than Thy word.
Give unto me as much as I may live on in peace,
And none turns away hungry

Your body, through prayer and affirmation, is willing itself back to its pure self, back to God, and out of the illusion that you have created. Remember, this whole experience we call life is an illusion created by you and only you can vacate the illusion and return to your God-self.

In contemplating prayers that have been with us for ages, prayers we invoke regularly in some form by many faiths, we can draw on the energy the prayer evokes to the many who repeat it. This *energy* stays present from the original source and sage who began its devotion. The familiar *Lord's Prayer* is one such entreaty that falls into this category. There are many more. The prayer attributed to St. Francis is another. Read carefully what St. Francis of Assisi (1182–1226) gave us so as to grasp and internalize the significance and power of prayer, as well as his choice on how to live—a lesson for all.

Lord, make me an instrument of your peace
Where there is hatred, let me sow love
Where there is injury, pardon;
Where there is doubt, faith;
Where there is despair, hope;
Where there is darkness, light;
And where there is sadness, joy.
O Divine Master, grant that I many not so much seek
To be consoled, as to console;
To be understood as to understand;
To be loved as to love;
For it is in giving that we receive;
It is in pardoning that we are pardoned;
And it is in dying that we are born to eternal light.

All of us at one time or another have invoked prayers of healing for a loved one. Those who are nurturers—mothers and fathers, for example—or other caring individuals, most often pray not for themselves, but for their cherished loved ones. They pray for a child with pain suffering injuries or disease, or a seemingly helpless or terminally ill friend or relative. Some of us send prayers to those who are suffering in natural tragedies, earthquakes, fires, tsunamis, and the like. Most of us feel helpless when these events occur and deep inside want to do something. We want to help alleviate the suffering of others, in some way. Many send money, practical aid, or choose to volunteer or contribute in whatever they can physically or appropriately do. All of us, however, may send prayers. We can do that even if we cannot contribute in a tangible way. The wondrous glory of the act of prayer is to actually know, truly know, that prayer is effective when it emanates from the heart and is sent with love.

How do we know that? How do we know that prayer actually works? Recent research has focused on prayer as a *practical* tool for healing. There are current documented studies of the phenomenon known as *non-local* healing that has awakened the healing power in many of us. Larry Dossey. M.D., a well respected and nationally known author and authority on spiritual healing, has researched several double blind studies wherein group prayer was directed at a select group of individuals and not for another group of individuals with the same general symptoms. You might well guess the results. The group receiving direct prayers had significantly more healing than the control group.[2] Such profound results are bringing us to new understandings of prayer, power and quantum abilities.

Dr. Dossey certainly had his share of fearful detractors. He quotes a *respected* scientist who blatantly stated, "That is the sort of thing I would not believe, even if it were true."[3] Dossey's well researched and documented response points out that in the 1600s, Isaac Newton was inventing new terms himself as he was attempting to figure out the universe. Newton invented the commonly accepted term, *gravity*, but had no knowledge of how it worked. The overwhelming accumulated data, Newton said, made it *mandatory* to propose the existence of gravity. How his fearful opponents thought the world ought to behave was irrelevant to Newton. He was severely ridiculed for his thought on his new term. Today, gravity is common knowledge—not because we now understand it, we still don't know how it works—we just have gotten used to it.[4]

I know for some of us this may sound like hocus pocus or mumbo jumbo, and defies the apparent *reality* of the physical and mental pain and suffering that we *witness* continually. There is no question that in this world and in our human form, we continually endure and witness pain and suffering. Most of humanity has accepted those conditions as our reality. In order to break from the confines of this old thinking, one needs to begin to view pain from a spiritual perspective and as a separate ego body in and of itself—or as Eckert Tolle labels it, the *pain body*.[5] Our ego has allowed our pain body to dictate the condition of our lives. Our quest is to stay in the NOW where the ego cannot dominate or survive, and where pain and suffering, the tools of the ego, can die also.

WORKS CITED

1. Singh, Kirpal, *Prayer,* Pg. 1
2. Dossey, Larry, *Reinventing Medicine,* pg 34
3. *Ibid*, pg. 34
4. *Ibid*, pg. 84
5. Tolle, Eckhart, *The Power of Now*, pg.36

CHAPTER 7

WHAT IS MEDITATION?

Ow MANY EYES do you have? A silly question you say? If you haven't suffered loss of vision or other eye trauma, you probably would answer, "two." In the outer physical world the answer you give would be considered, of course, obvious and correct. However, there is another eye—just above the bridge of your nose set back between your two eyes and acknowledged by sages and spirits and all who have traveled inward, as the third eye.

While not a physical eye, this is the eye that opens so you may see the *inner* world, the *non-illusionary* world—indeed, the vision of your soul. We learn to open the third eye through *meditation*, the other communication tool along with prayer we possess that connects us to God.

Knowing what meditation is and how it works will help you understand the tools mankind has to communicate with his inner self, communicate with God. Meditation is the key to hearing truth, knowing truth and tapping into your natural intuition. Mantras, which I will talk about later, are highly effective tools to help still and quiet the mind for meditation.

So exactly what is meditation? In simple language it means,

Stilling the mind and practicing to drive our conscious thoughts out of our mind and leave it open for the divine sound and light that is always there to be heard or seen.

Meditation is the conduit for God's messages to you. It is a simple practice, but not necessarily a rapid sojourn that grants instant rewards. Of course, the rapidity of its effectiveness is relative for each of us depending where each is spiritually. Meditation must be patiently and diligently practiced. For many of us, it will take some time, much dedication, and continuing perseverance to realize the long-term benefits. The immediate reward, however, is the realization of the abundant yielding of the silent calmness within that opens your mind, gradually, to see and hear the inner truths.

J. Krishnamurti, a 20th century sage from India, who brought his teachings to the West in the mid 20th century, approached meditation in this way.

The highest form of sensitivity with the brain completely still is the quality of love. Love is a most extraordinary thing if you have it in your heart. Love is not pleasure. Love has nothing to do with fear. It is not related to sex. It is the quality of the mind that is free, sensitive, intelligent with the brain not responding in terms of the past...and

therefore, still. Then the heart comes upon this perfume
called love. The understanding of that is meditation. That
is the foundation of meditation.[1]

Young Siddartha Gautama was the privileged Asian prince who
forsook his lofty station and riches and wandered the countryside
searching for the real truth and meaning of life. He spent his years
in meditation under the fabled Bhodi tree and became known as
the *Buddha, or Enlightened One.* Perhaps you have knowledge of
another yogi, swami, guru or sage who did the same—meditating
for years in their attempt to reach and understand enlightenment.
There are many today deeply committed to enlightenment that
spends much of their being in meditation. Without getting into the
history of those souls, let's recognize and affirm that meditation *is*
a sure path of enlightenment.

Enlightenment is also a journey, not necessarily just
a destination, but a sure path to peace, serenity, joy, and
understanding. All of us have this capability within and available
to us, but only if we take the time, apply the energy and have
the patience to sit, practice, and allow the light and sound, the
language of God, to come to you, through you. We cannot easily
hear the spiritual siren if we are living in our noisy, conscious
world of relativity. We are much too distracted. Some refer to this
distraction phenomenon as the workings of our conscious thoughts,
our *monkey mind*, constantly swinging from thought to thought
without the pondering of spirit.

We are often unaware of what is happening in our minds.
Sometimes we choose unawareness by ingesting mind altering drugs
or continually following our ego's desires. Our bodies, however,
seek balance. We can always rebalance by bringing awareness back
to ourselves through meditation. When we have connection to

awareness, we naturally create balance. Our minds, led by our egos, tend to go back and forth from past to the future, rehashing the past and rehearsing the future. Some have described this as *jumping from history to mystery.* We generally have no clue that our personal story is continually running like a B movie in the background of our daily lives, complete with previews and reviews. It is essential to have the Mind STOP. It is essential, however, to first *intend it* to stop. It is necessary to seek peace from the distracting world and allow yourself to be in the NOW. When you are in the NOW, you are achieving it through a form of meditation.

Occasionally, sound and light does come through in spite of the distractions. By the miracle of intuition, guidance comes through our soul and is not attributable to our bodies or brain. It is, however, only when we quiet our ego and calm our egocentric minds that we are able to open the third eye and connect within. It is only when we choose to welcome silence that we are able to begin and sustain our journey. It is only when we are in a state of allowing spirit to enter that we reap the rewards of meditation.

The external world is a constant jamming device; static that corrupts sound and light, distorting its inward receptors and compelling us to remain in the domain of the ego. Attempting to corral the ego and quiet its effects upon us is part of our seemingly daunting mission. It doesn't mean we shouldn't pay attention to our outer, physical world, but it does mean that we should gradually learn to withdraw from the chains that bind us to the birth and death cycle that keeps us from ascending into the higher dimensions and welcoming light. It is in those higher dimensions where true freedom exists. One of the great mystics and sages of our time, Lord Shiva, the Hindu saint, gave heedsome advice about the process of meditating and the relationship to the external world. He said:

Try to penetrate as deeply as you can into your mind, keep moving inwards but do not forget the realities of the external world, because if you ignore the external realities, your internal peace will also be disturbed.[2]

Another sage from the Orient, Chuang-Tse, said this about meditation,

When we become interested in meditation, it is a sign that we are ready to take the journey to another level. As long as the journey remains an outer one, the real goal of our endeavors is never in sight. We continue looking out there for our destination, never realizing that the "I" that is doing the looking is what we are actually looking for.[3]

We could discuss hundreds, perhaps thousands, of sage examples regarding meditation from those who have extensively traveled the inward journey. It is today grounded into our very being and has taken root throughout the world, from its ancient birthplace in the Orient to the modern frontiers of the West.

One of the meditating tools used by many is the *mantra*. How many of us understand the history and function of a mantra? The mantra has a rich spiritual history that has permeated meditation throughout the millenniums. Perhaps those of us in the modern *baby boomer* generation relate mantras back to past experiences of dodging young men and women with shaved heads, dressed in saffron colored robes at various airports while they were mouthing some seemingly incomprehensible babble. Later, when we took time to listen and learn, we translated the so-called babble to *Hare Krishna*, a mantra used by the sect to keep them connected with God being while raising money and supporters to sustain their quest to change the world. They became somewhat infamous as a sect, a butt of jokes, and generated many varied opinions centering on their alleged weirdness and audacity. Their use of a mantra was not highly appreciated by the airport's busy customers. The West, however, was just waking up to Eastern spirituality and similar practices embraced by the Hare Krishnas and others. Were they the vanguards of eastern spiritual awareness and awakening in the United States even as they tended to irritate the traveling masses?

In truth, mantras were akin to the first thoughts that appeared in many ancient religious scriptures, including the Christian Bible. "In the beginning was the Word, and the Word was of God," is the familiar biblical phrase that most of us have learned. *The Tibetan Book of the Dead* describes reality as "reverberating like a thousand distant thunders." *Mantra* is a Sanskrit word that is translated as *"that which liberates the mind."* In a syllabic breakdown, *Man* equals 'mind' and *tra* means 'freedom.' It therefore can be defined as a group of charged words that when meditated upon will lead the mind to freedom. It has the power to help us dissolve our conscious thoughts, detour our "monkey brain," and open the door to the inner spirit.

In virtually all ancient scriptures, sound was identified as the initial force in the creation of the universe. Mantras have that unique connection as a repetition of the primordial sound of creation. The words may be different as delivered to disciples from their respective masters, but all have the connection that is transmitted by the teachers, through a long lineage of teachers, throughout man's history on this earth. As such, they carry a charged message from the beginning—the Word.

Mantras originated and are based from the initial universal sound, *Aum or Om*.[4] *Om* carries the ancient sound message from the beginning of time and reminds us to calm the outer world distractions and allow ourselves to enter and connect with the realm of God through meditation. Sound is *energy*, and energy is the foundation of *all that is*. Sound vibrations are the energy *stuff* of the universe as each organism and object emits its own unique and special energetic vibrational footprint. Much like tuning your radio dial, we only hear the sounds when we focus on a particular station, or sound vibration. The purpose of a mantra is of itself a distraction device. Repeating a mantra assists the meditator to ground oneself without laboriously chasing random thoughts from one's mind.

Mantras should be repeated slowly, without mouthing of the lips, usually in silence, yet can be spoken aloud as a channeling device through chanting. However, following your spirit guide or teacher's instruction should take precedent in regards as to how the practice should be executed.

Each guru, teacher, swami or sage may have a special mantra that is handed down from generation to generation. A living master, a complete soul-man, passes the wisdom of the words and secret down to his chosen disciple who passes it on further to the next generation of masters. As the disciples grow in number, the mantra becomes less a secret but doesn't lose its divine power granted from the master soul.

One would consider a mantra as a *focal point* allowing confused and disjointed thoughts to melt away and be replaced by bypassing the conscious and subconscious mind to activate the *superconscious* mind—the mind of God. This new awareness takes the form of oneness with the cosmos, or a unifying and loving experience with the inner-self through the superconscious. Scientists are calling this the fourth state of consciousness. In its most basic sense, meditation allows us to quiet the emotions, control the mind, and relax the physical body. This is the key. It is up to us to manifest the key to unlock the spiritual gate.

WORKS CITED

1. Krishnamurti. J., *Meeting Life*, pg. 168

2. Shiva was one of the gods of the Vedas

3. While there is some question as to whether Chuang Tse actually existed, his philosophy on meditation is reflected in a work consisting of 33 chapters.

4. OM, Aum, or (Onkar) in Sikh theology translates to "as a symbol of God, God is one, a singular God and is considered the universal sound or the "word." It is said to be the original sound that contains all other sounds, all words, all languages and all mantras.

   AMEN purportedly shares some roots with the Sanskrit word OM or AUM. It roughly translates to "so be it truly," found in the Hebrew Bible and New Testament. Jesus often used AMEN to put emphasis on his own word—translated as "verily" (see Isaiah 65:16)

CHAPTER 8

WHAT IS THE *EGO?*

"We have met the enemy and he is us"
—Pogo

Y OU WILL NOTICE that in the chapter title above, the word *ego* is emphasized. That is by design. The exterior view of ourselves in this physical world usually manifests as an entity whose primary identification is with that incredible, egotistical, self-serving, personal pronoun—I.

I, referred to here as ego, is the lowest level of consciousness in the universal mind and is the single most negative entity that keeps us trapped in the physical world of recycled suffering. We may think that *I* is a wonderful and powerful concept, because we tend to congratulate ourselves when we satisfy the ego and aggrandize those traits that purport to lift us above others—supposedly allowing ourselves to feel superior, thus better.

By allowing ego to determine our life path, we deactivate the power of intention that exists as a force in the universe.

Ego, according to *Wayne Dyer*,[1] is made up of six primary ingredients that account for how we experience ourselves as disconnected. Here is how the ego defines us.

1) *I am what I own.* I am defined by my possessions. The more material possessions I tend to accumulate, the more power I seem to have. If my possessions define who I am, then the popular *bumper sticker* philosophy, *He who has the most toys, wins,* becomes the quest. Such an illusionary victory! Surely we know we can't take any material things with us to the next level. Nothing material we acquire has any spiritual worth. The ego tries to convince us otherwise.

2) *I am what I do.* Who I am is defined by my achievements in this life. Another folly presented by the ego. One's achievements, job status, position, accomplishments in the material sense, seem to give rise to false pride and personal gratification. None of our "accomplishments" are truly valid, at least not in the spiritual realm. Those accomplishments only have power if they lead you to a spiritual understanding or solution. Again, you can't take your achievements with you.

3) *I am what others think of me.* I am defined by my reputation. In the clockwork schematic universe, however, what others think of us is absolutely immaterial. Our spiritual mission comes from Source and our reputation is a personal challenge that only we, while understanding our spiritual mission, can grow from. If one follows his heart, his intuition, the choices

he makes are valid and will survive the apparent judgment of others. You are the only judge of you. It is always *your* choice to define your reputation, not the choice of others.

4) *I am separate from everyone.* This is the belief that my corporeal existence, my body, is defined by ego as alone and separate. There is no other, no spirit guide that directs my path. When we get down to basic physics, we know that all of us, each of us, is made up of the same stuff; atoms, space and energy. What we forget is that we are the key to our own vibrations which sets us seemingly apart from each other. In truth, the universe is geared to vibrate as one; one universe—representing many parts. This is analogous to our own cells which seemingly act and vibrate independently, yet cooperately facilitate the whole body. We are one. Only the ego suggests that we are separate. The ego has a very limited 5 senses point of view.

5) *I am separate from all that is missing from my life.* In other words, my life space is disconnected from my desires. Everything seems to happen by chance and there is no grand plan. *The Chaos Theory* operates on this plane even as quantum physics has shown this so-called theory of a chaotic universe to be false. The ego loves this chaotic scenario and perpetuates it to convince us that desire is in conflict with true reality. *Stuff happens* and we accept that as truth. That's the definition of chaos. Nothing could be further from the truth. Our consciousness determines our desires and it is connected directly to God or the Source. It is the same force that Carlos Castaneda suggests is the basis of intention. It is always there but depends on us to activate that desire. We must remember

that the universe is a marvelous, magnificent, and precise place, operating like clockwork where chaos cannot and does not exist.

The moment we realize that we are always connected to Source and all our desires are intertwined with Source, it is in that infinite thought that we realize that we are NEVER separate from that which is missing in our lives. We need only to tap into that consciousness to activate our desires.

6) *I am separate from God.* Ego tells us that our lives depend on God's assessment of our worthiness. This may come as a shock to many, but God does not judge. He just loves. You needn't be a *God-fearing* mortal. If he were to judge, he would have to live in a relative world and not the divine and infinite world. He would be *limited* and subject to extremes of love and fear. Love does not contain those relative extremes and God is love. Our lives are an illusion and not subject to worthiness or unworthiness. How can we limit the infinite by defining God with our own illusionary concepts and thus laying on him our illusionary finite fears? If we choose to accept that we must be worthy in order to ascend to enlightenment, then we continually deny the love of God, the work of the universe.

Those acquired traits; fame, beauty, ability, status, wealth or other such egotistical acquisitions, give us our self-serving identities. We love that, don't we? We tend to love thinking of ourselves above and superior to the great unwashed masses, however defined. Feeding the ego seems to be the most satisfying act that most of us enjoy doing.

Feeding the voracious and insatiable appetite of the ego, however, proves to be an unappeasable chore. It becomes the "elephant in the room" that we seemingly choose to ignore. In truth, our main challenge is to gather the will to confront the appetite of the ego and gradually moderate its influence until we are able to either eliminate it completely or relegate it to a very minor role serving us in the 3rd dimension. We must learn to have a partnership with the ego that allows the ego to assist us in functioning in this world while not dominating our existence. Those traits we do not address or resolve in this lifetime become a virtual rain check for yet another attempt in yet another life, until we reconcile our addiction to them. Quite a chore, yet one we all must face and accept if we are to follow the path of the *Lightseeker*.

The ego can provide us with an enticing slow-dance, complete with a host of appeasing qualities—qualities that we must learn to temper if we are to welcome in the light. According to *A Course in Miracles,* we truly must understand the *ego's* dance and how it *can* be undone. Eckert Tolle has introduced the concept of the previously mentioned "pain body." The pain body becomes the manifestation of the conflict that the ego tries so desperately to preserve. Tolle goes on to explain:

> *The ego always tries to preserve conflict. It is very ingenious in devising ways that seem to diminish conflict, because it does not want you to find conflict so intolerable that you will insist on giving it up. The ego, therefore tries to persuade you that it can free you of conflict, lest you give the ego up and free yourself. Using its own warped version of the laws of God, the ego utilizes the power of the mind only to defeat the mind's real purpose. It projects conflict from your mind to other minds, in an attempt to persuade you that you have gotten rid of the problem.[2]*

A *Course In Miracles* says that the ego's conflict cannot be projected to another because it cannot be shared. You own it! Any attempt to keep part of it and get rid of another part does not really mean anything. The teachings of the *Course* emphasizes that the ego is a conflicted teacher, and a conflicted teacher is a poor teacher—and a poor learner. Ego's lessons are confused, and its transfer value is limited by its confusion. You can't give conflict away. Trying to give it away is how the ego keeps it. The ego's belief is that by seeing the conflict outside, *you have excluded it from within.* That is a complete distortion of the power of extension.

People's egos are afraid that their projections of conflict will return and hurt them. If they believe that their egos have blotted their projections from their own mind, they also believe that the projections are trying to creep back in. The dilemma is such that the egos projections have not left our minds, and the ego is forced to engage in constant activity in order *not* to recognize this.

In truth, one cannot perpetuate an illusion about another without perpetuating it about oneself self. A *Course in Miracles* says:

There is no way out of this, because it is impossible to fragment the mind. To fragment is to break into pieces, and mind cannot attack or be attacked. The belief that it can, an error that the ego always makes, underlies its whole use of projection. It does not understand what mind is, and therefore does not understand what you are. Yet its existence is dependent on your mind, because the ego is your belief. The ego is confusion in identification. Never having a consistent model, it never developed consistently. It is the product of misapplication of the laws of God by distorted minds that are misusing their power.[3]

It follows that, according to the *Course in Miracles*, the whole *purpose of our spiritual quest* is to learn that the ego is unbelievable and will forever be unbelievable. When you are in ego, you are not in your true self. One cannot *be* in one's true self and still be in the ego. It is *absolutely* in conflict with the realization of your true self. The following quote from Paramahansa Yogananda (1893–1952) illuminates this point.

> *Man has falsely identified himself with the pseudo-soul or ego. When he transfers his sense of identity to his true being, the immortal Soul, he discovers that all pain is unreal. He no longer can even imagine the state of suffering.*[4]

The key that unlocks this circle is to be in presence, to be in the NOW. The ego cannot be in the present. It only exists in the illusionary residue of your mind as the past, which is gone forever, or the future, which has not arrived.

That is the gift of the beautiful and healing role of meditation and prayer. When we still the mind, we dissolve the ego and open ourselves to the true existence of the soul, our true selves. It is here, in the silence, where God hangs out waiting for you to come to him. He keeps the door open. All you have to do is give it a gentle nudge and enter. This is as true today as it was hundreds of years ago as expressed in the following:

Look to this day
For it is life
The very life of life.
In its brief course lie
All the realities and verities of existence:
The bliss of growth,
The splendor of action,
The glory of power.
For yesterday is but a dream
And tomorrow is only a vision.
But today, well lived,
Makes every yesterday a dream of happiness
And every tomorrow a vision of hope.
Look well therefore to this day.
—Kalidasa, fourth-century Indian playwright

So how do we summarize what ego is and where it originates? Let us understand that it is truly representative of a separate creature—the combination of the conscious and subconscious mind. The ego is an intangible mechanism within a human being that stimulates his or her mannerisms and characteristics translating them into outer actions and reactions under one's individual life condition. Those mannerisms and attributes are established from all of one's past incarnation experiences, the varied experiences of this incarnation, and one's attitude toward these experiences.

Enlightened people, or those who seem to be enlightened, can appear to be ego-less, but what they have actually done is to remove the ego from the pilot's seat, so to speak, and relegate it to the passenger's seat where it actually belongs. The ego only serves as a vehicle for expressing ourselves in the third dimension. If we were entirely without ego, we would have difficulty functioning properly in this dimension.

According to Vedic tradition, an individual takes this ego with him or her in other planes and expressions of the conscious and subconscious mind—changing and building as one goes.

Therein, again, lay the element of choice. Either we choose to follow the false ego, replete with all its limitations and illusions, and continue the illusion that it habitually presents, or we still the egoic mind and enter the superconscious God-mind and begin the process of exiting the seemingly interminable wheel of birth, death and rebirth on this physical plane. The gift of free will to each of us governs which path we will take. Again, the choice is ours. It always is.

Works Cited

1.   Dyer, Dr. Wayne, *The Power of Intention*, pg. 10

2.   *A Course in Miracles*, pg.130

3.   *A Course in Miracles*

4.   Yogananda, Paramahansa, *Where There Is Light*, pg. 20

CHAPTER 9

WHAT POWER DOES
FORGIVENESS GIVE US?

The weak can never forgive.
Forgiveness is the attribute of the strong.

—*Mohandas K. Ghandi*

GHANDI HAD IT RIGHT. To forgive, one must have the fortitude, compassion, and discipline, as the bible says, "to turn the other cheek." Ghandi taught his followers the power of non-violence and forgiveness and with that changed a country's destiny and gave the world a lesson in spiritual strength. After seeing the changes he strove for, he extended his passion to reflect forgiveness, compassion, and love for all those who confronted his principles.

The great civil rights leader of the 1960s, Martin Luther King, Jr., said,

> *We must develop and maintain the capacity to forgive. He who is devoid of the power to forgive is devoid of the power to love. There is some good in the worst of us and some evil in the best of us. When we discover this, we are less prone to hate our enemies.*

King's passion for forgiveness allowed the masses that followed his teachings to change forever the direction of prejudice, not only in his home in the United States, but his influence fostered loving changes and hope throughout the world.

Forgiveness is a practice that involves a fearless intention to uncover the layers and work through the web of painful thoughts stored deep within the subconscious mind. As you work through each feeling or thought that arises, you learn that the process of forgiving others inevitably brings you back to forgiving yourself. You come to recognize the role your own thoughts played in inviting the situation, or at the very least, in allowing the situation or event to occur through a lack of awareness.

In moving through the forgiveness process, you go beyond the pain and embrace every experience as a step in your learning. You then move on, knowing you have acquired new skills and are capable of creating better and more fulfilling experiences.

Forgiveness goes hand in hand with spirit. With this attribute man has the intrinsic power to transform himself and his brethren to a heavenly peace here on this earth. "Ah, if it were only so simple," we all cry out! Yet it truly is simple. Imagine for a moment if each and every one of us practiced daily the act of forgiveness and expressed the grail of gratitude for what is rather than to dictate what one "wishes" it to be. Conflict would virtually disappear. Understanding and compassion would be the norm. Judgment would be a distant memory and life would be sweetened with bliss, love, and respect. I love to again quote my favorite comic strip character, Pogo, a curious but now defunct anthropomorphic "possum" who stated with conviction and irony, "We have met the enemy and he is us." Such a profound assertion from a comic strip character that was always fun and philosophical! Yes, we are or can be our own worst enemy when it comes to forgiveness. It doesn't have to be that way, not with the inner strength and power we possess.

Deepak Chopra defines this concept as the *Law of Least Effort* and presents this application for practice. He says,

> *I will practice acceptance. Today I will accept people, situations, circumstances, and events as they occur. I will know that this moment is as it should be, because the whole universe is as it should be. I will not struggle against the whole universe by struggling against this moment. My acceptance is total and complete. I accept things as they are this moment, not as I wish they were.*[2]

Chopra knows that accepting what is, and not struggling with what we cannot immediately change, is the key to changing our attitudes, our relationships and our situations when we prepare ourselves spiritually with the expression of love for all. To Chopra, acceptance means looking past what is physically obvious in behaviors and appearance and focus instead on the *real* souls that reside in these imperfect bodies. By affirming his commitment to practicing acceptance, Chopra teaches us that accepting others and forgiving them for what they appear to be, lights the path to enlightenment. When expressing acceptance and forgiveness, others will delight in your reflective warmth and be given the unspoken opportunity to willingly forgive you as well. Peace and love become immediately evident in these relationships. Both of you are mutually expressing the overarching love that permeates the universe. A sense of power, well-being, and love becomes ingrained in your thoughts and embedded in your soul—the basic *stuff* of ascension.

Jack Kornfield, a noted spiritual author trained as a Buddhist monk, quotes a wonderful story of two former prisoners of war: When one asked, "Have you forgiven your captors?" the other replied, "No, never." The first ex-prisoner looked with kindness at his friend and said, "Well, then they still have you in prison, don't they." [3]

"To forgive," Kornfield goes on to say, *"We must face the pain and sorrow of our betrayal and disappointment, and discover the movement of the heart that opens to forgive in spite of it all...each of us will find our hearts closed or feel ourselves hostage to the past at times during our journey."* [4]

No one is implying that it is easy. Remember, in this world we are all teachers and we are all students and we are all one. Forgiveness is a wonderful teacher.

Matthew Fox, noted author and spiritual teacher, says that forgiveness is another word for *Letting go.* He says that *forgiveness is a learned drip by drip process, day by day, not as an act of altruism, but as a necessary cleansing of the past, a purification of our souls so we can live and function effectively in the now."* [5] He suggests that one cannot grow one's soul into its full potential when it harbors past hurts and turns them over and over. Doing so would be to enable and grow bitterness, not soul.

J. Krishnamurti said, "...*the consciousness of each one of us is the consciousness of the rest of the world. And if there is a radical change in that consciousness, that consciousness will affect the rest of the world.*" [6]

So yes, we have the mission and the ability to change the world through our forgiveness.

So how do we begin to learn to forgive? First, of course, one has to have the capacity and desire to forgive oneself. This can become the initial and perhaps largest obstacle in forgiving and accepting others. But, as Deepak Chopra suggests, the process begins with you. It can only begin with you as we are all one.

As we as individuals shed the burden of our past painful memories, we discover and come to identify with the eternal "I" that exists beyond our current story. We begin to incorporate forgiveness as a way of thinking and behaving in the world. More than being an action or activity, forgiveness becomes an approach to life in each moment. It is then that we discover what true freedom really means.

And with this newfound freedom we can begin to live our forgiveness. As we approach others in our daily lives, we now have the desire and capacity to look beyond and through our initial impressions and habitual observations and see with a new set of eyes. We are able to see with more clarity the inner soul of each of our fellow brethren and observe how our initial impression begins to dissipate. Now we can behold them as the *holy encounter* that we are presented. It could be a simple smile or acknowledgement of his or her presence. With our gift of forgiveness, we bring light to others as it is reflected from within. In turn, we ignite the natural love that is within others and gift them with the ability to pass it on. With forgiveness from each of us to others, we light up the world and bring peace and love to all its inhabitants.

A beautiful passage from *A Course in Miracles* gives us the strength and guidance of the power of forgiveness:

> *Do you want peace? Forgiveness offers it.*
> *Do you want happiness, a quiet mind,*
> *a certainty of purpose,*
> *and a sense of worth and beauty*
> *that transcends the world?*
> *Do you want a quietness that cannot be disturbed,*
> *a gentleness that can never be hurt,*
> *a deep abiding comfort,*
> *and a rest so perfect it can never be upset?*
> *All this forgiveness offers you*

Works Cited

1.   Elizabeth, Annie, Affirmations for Everyday Living, pg. 7
2.   Chopra, Deepack, The Seven Spiritual Laws of Success, pg. 63
3.   Kornfield, Jack, After the Ecstasy, The Laundry, Pg. 47
4.   Ibid, Pg. 47
5.   Fox, Matthew, The Hidden Spirituality of Men, pg. 94
6.   Krishnamurti, J., Meeting Life, pg. 174

CHAPTER 10

WHY IS GRATITUDE A PATH TO THE SOURCE?

Gratitude is not only the greatest of virtues,
but the parent of all the others.
—Cicero

Gratitude is a way of expressing your appreciation of
the Universal Mind, sending a message of what it is you
would like to have more of in life.
—Annie Elizabeth, *Affirmations for Everyday Living*

Gratitude is a key spiritual courtesy, no less important
and beneficial than showing gratitude and courtesy to
others in our everyday lives. It is appreciated by the soul
world no less than it is by your fellow human beings.
—Zhi Gang Sha, Soul, Mind, Body Medicine

Send gratitude through your body: bring to mind something
in your life about which you can feel thankful. Gratitude
is among the most profound spiritual healers. Send this
feeling of gratitude through your body. Say thank you
to your heart, your lungs, your kidneys, all your organs.
Thank your legs for walking you. Make it a practice to
focus several times each day on feelings of gratitude.
—Donna Eden, *Energy Medicine*

EACH DAY WHEN we awaken, we open our eyes, smell the scents of morning and feel the dawning of another miraculous opportunity. It is a miracle to be aware of a new day, aware of a new start and full of hope for another day of living. The act of recognizing such a gift is the first opportunity for us in the awareness of gratitude. We might have fallen asleep the night before with stress, angst, anger, or fear dominating our thoughts. Even so, how can we not be grateful for the overnight respite and awaking another day and have the opportunity to choose love and peaceful living in our lives?

With the morning comes a new beginning, a rebirth of you, of your spirit. How can we not be grateful for yet another moment in this world to grasp the opportunity to be grateful.

All of life is truly a gift. Every person you may encounter in the course of your day is a present to you from God. It is a natural scenario presented moment to moment from Source to you to exercise your opportunity to choose and give of yourself the gift of love while receiving love in return for your giving. Many choose to recognize these moments as *Holy Encounters*.

When we awaken in the morning we are waiting to say our morning blessing, *Good Morning!* to all who will listen, and to wait in anticipation for the expected reciprocal response from those we love. Each of us expresses gratitude that we are acknowledged and a morning salutation is the opening gamut for the first day of the rest of our lives. Assured of an initial boost to a good day, we are instantly grateful to be who and what we are.

It has been said that the only true prayer is that of gratitude, not of supplication or desire. Gratitude is the first step to giving and receiving. The lyrics of a once popular song begins, "When I'm worried and I can't sleep, I count my blessing instead of sheep, and I fall asleep counting my blessings." Sometimes we find great truths making themselves obvious in axioms, poems and song lyrics. I wonder how closely we pay attention to these subliminal messages?

So many of us find ourselves struggling through the day building up stress, focusing on what fears or problems we are currently experiencing, or projecting the fears into what lies ahead. We seldom pause and express our gratitude or count our blessings, instead fretting and worrying ourselves without taking time to realize how much we do have, how fortunate we are.

When we are feeling grateful we are actuating ourselves in the Now or present. We are telling Source what we want by gratitude and asking for more. That is, of course, what our spiritual quest is all about—learning to live in the present moment. Ego, a persistent negative companion, cannot exist in the present moment. This is why gratitude is important. It is a tool enabling us to feel what it's like to be in this moment. Gratitude is always heart opening feelings. We can feel our heart and chest opening and expanding in gratitude because they are qualities of our divine origin.

Gratitude is a feeling that leads to incredibly powerful connections between us and divine Source and nature. It calls forth a huge download of energy that floods into our crown chakra[1] and fills up our body space and aura.

Gratitude is the humble expression of the soul that allows spirit to connect with the mind and body. As a *Lightseeker* develops the habit of exhibiting gratitude, the action becomes ingrained in the physical body, thus freeing the body from the continual and illusionary trappings of the ego. As one detaches oneself from the ego's manifestations, one's life work shifts to being grateful for what *is* and is directed to the service of others. Make no mistake about this; service to others is also service to oneself. We are indeed all one and our graciousness and service to others is service to one's own soul. *A Course in Miracles* says; "All that we give is given to ourselves."

We know that gratitude is the first step to receiving and experiencing a miraculous and magical journey. We should consider it an affirmation to experience and grow our faith and knowledge. We must learn to appreciate everything that we already have. If we can learn to love the present moment while we are in the present moment, we enter into a place of calmness and in a position to enjoy the gifts contained in the present moment. Eastern philosophy refers to this practice of focusing our thoughts as *Zen*. In this Zen space of NOW, we can achieve that special connection with Source. We then are free to move and rapidly grow in the direction that we desire.

In short, gratitude for all things in the past, present, and future works the wonders of the universe. It is the energy pack that we utilize to recharge our universal connection.

WORKS CITED

1.   Chakras (wheels). In Yoga, the seven occult centers of life and consciousness in the spine and brain, which enliven the physical and astral bodies of man. Referred to as chakras because the concentrated energy in each one is like a hub from which radiate rays of life-giving light and energy.

CHAPTER 11

GOOD & EVIL, FREE WILL, & CHOICE?

We choose our joys and sorrows long
before we experience them.
—Kahlil Gibran

T HE STORY OF mankind throughout time has asked the dualistic questions; what is good and what is evil? How do we choose which path is either? Without a doubt, this has been one of the most persistent problems of understanding for all of us. Philosophers throughout the ages have wrestled with the question, each giving his/her particular opinion and declaring the problem solved—only to find that the question has risen again by others with yet another vested answer. As newer thoughts advanced, the question became much more complicated and modern philosophers have added to or reinterpreted their predecessor's theories.

So the persistent question lingers to this day. Is there an absolute, ultimate, and unquestioned measure of good and evil that will stand the test of time until time is no more?

If one were to examine The Ten Commandments of the ancient Hebrews, one would find an example of two extremes. One extreme suggests the Commandments were strict statements of eternal law handed down from God to Moses and spoke the authority of the commandments for all times and all places. Good and evil are absolute.

The other extreme is from those who postulate that both good and evil are relative to the conditions of a particular time and place. For instance, they would suggest that good and evil acts and thoughts can easily be identified in one place and time, but the same acts or thought defined as good or evil in that one place would not necessarily be identified as such in another place, time, or condition.

Throughout history mankind has tussled with this seemingly perplexing problem (perhaps not so perplexing to some as each philosophy swears by its own interpretation). We tend to ask the companion question that fosters some disbelief in Source; *How can an all-good God create a world where there are these apparent evils?*

It would appear that we have been approaching the *problem* of good and evil as a logical, sequential, finite and, as a certainly timeless and controversial question. Those who believe that the Ten Commandments come directly from God interpret those codes literally, rather than compromising an understanding of what they have acknowledged to believe to be the true meaning. Those on the opposite extreme maintain an abject dismissal of such literal interpretation and believe that good and evil are relative. Mankind has thus been polarized and steeped in the free will of interpreting the concept of good and evil.

With all of this in mind, and in order to offer a different spiritual perspective, let's take an ethereal trip into that space that exists between time. On this trip, we will consider the reality of reincarnation and the connection we have with our co-creating spirit or Source. Let's look at another way to approach the question, "How did I get here?"

For this moment, consider yourself having gone through a requisite number of incarnations, in that *pre-life*—between the life before you incarnated into this life. Imagine that in this space-place between lives, we have the ability to choose our existence and experiences and we chose (created) this current life—indeed created this body, this earth, this galaxy and so on as the co-creators that we are. Suppose still that we created this life in order to learn or relearn the lessons (to get off the eternal wheel) that we have not yet learned and/or assimilated from our many previous lifetimes.

Let's further assume that in this co-creation with spirit, we gave ourselves free will to act as we choose while in this corporeal body. Remember, we are co-creating with Source. We also provided ourselves in this creation with some choices to make, while allowing that *we would __not__ be able to know that we had free will __or consciously remember__ the lessons or activities of our previous lives.* In fact, in this pre-life, we make the choice to forget any past life or lesson, except for some vague and foggy memories that linger because our spirit selves acknowledged the need to start over and address our unlearned lesson(s) again—perhaps in a different setting, time, and place or perhaps on a different world. We also choose, in that space between lives, not to remember so we may interact in the next life without any preconceived notions on how to utilize our free will. The free will that we bring into this new corporeal being is the main tool we can access to manifest our new reality and to exercise the ability to choose a potential alternate path, so we may evolve spiritually and not repeat our past poor choices. In the process of starting over, we now come equipped in our incarnation with our *pre-selected* choices that we knew in our pre-life and we use our gift of *apparent free will* in our new life to make those choices. I say apparent free will because we made many of our choices in our pre-life. We might well have chosen in our pre-life our geography, our families, friends, contacts with people and places we will live and the relationships we will engender. Consequently, in our pre-life when our spiritual vision was crystal clear, and we knew what we needed to progress to a higher spiritual realm, we chose our families, friends, and acquaintances as teachers, perhaps not necessarily all pleasant teachers with pleasant experiences, but teachers nevertheless. It might be argued that some of our *perceived enemies* may prove to be our most valued teachers. We chose them as our teachers—in order to give us the *opportunity* to change our thoughts and spiritual vibrations to conform to the lessons we sent ourselves here to learn. Our many incarnations are an indication of how often we don't choose to pay attention to those teachers or lessons.

We are thus *born again*, if you will excuse the political/religious use of this turn of phrase, and set out on our path to pursue our new life—*unmindful* of the lesson(s) we have chosen to incarnate in a physical body to learn. We must remember that *unmindfulness* was one our choices we conditioned in our pre-life. A knowledge of past life involvements would be perceived as "external" pressures that would prove inimical to development of disciplined free will in this lifetime. Therefore, that knowledge is, mercifully, denied to most of us at the conscious level. [1]

Yet there could well linger an ethereal memory from our past lives that is carried over to this life that haunts our dreams and thoughts. We aren't always sure we know what that is, but we often label it as *intuition*. We can assume that pre-life choices and spirit connection is where our sub-conscious human intuition comes from—a form of past life remembering that doesn't seem to necessarily reflect any actual current life physical experiences. Our ability to choose allows us to select new paths of relationship, purpose, and pursuit. We may very well, however, not pay attention to our intuition and continue to make the same repetitive choices again and again that will bring us back to this physical plane, again. We become mesmerized by the ego and seek those pleasures that we feel are real on the physical plane. We chose not to remember our own pre-choices in the now mysteriously forgotten space between incarnations, and those pre-choices dictate the pattern of our physical lives.

Life is all about choices. When we cut away the chaff, *every* situation is a choice. You choose how to react to situations. You choose how people affect your mood. You choose to be in a good mood or bad mood. In many ways you choose whether or not to be healthy. It's your choice how to live your life.

The question then becomes, "How do we make those choices that will enable us to exit the birth and death cycle and ascend to a higher spiritual plane, a choice that doesn't contain the relative evil we recognize here in our bodies, in the world, in this universe?" You will note that I used the term *relative evil*. I would also use the term *relative good* here. If these terms are relative, and they can only exist in a finite world, they cannot be infinite. They can only be finite creations of our mind. We live in a relative world. We have descended into our bodies from an infinite world. One is the real world, the other the relative world or, more succinctly, the illusionary world. Perhaps, when we examine the spiritual knowledge pertaining to this illusion, we are able to relate more directly to Plato's visionary analogy of the illusionary world projected on his cave wall.

So, how do we make the choice that enables us to exit the birth and death cycle? If we go deep inside, we tend to realize that avoiding that cycle is the pathway out.

The sages and mystics, yogis and prophets throughout history, including the religious messiahs of Abraham personified in Christianity, Judaism, and Islam, have all preached that the function of our minds is to experience love and to seek joy. And so the question we should ask ourselves is not "What is God, or who is God?," but "What is Love, or the ultimate expression of joy?"

The answer, perhaps, isn't as complicated as we might imagine. Love is the *energy* or *stuff* of the universe and is the *only* thing that is permanent and not an illusion. Studies in the quantum field have confirmed that when we think with Love, we can influence and change our lives and its destiny. When we think with Love, we are fulfilling our spiritual contract with our Source and are co-creating our existence with God. Buddha said, "All that is arises with our thoughts. With our thoughts, we make the world."

Only when we choose Love and joy with positive thoughts and actions do we fulfill our spirit and begin the journey on the path that leads us off the birth and death wheel. Those choices lead us through to the next level where our positive choosing enables our minds to experience the joy and to allow the spirit to guide us in fulfilling our contract with our soul. Our *intuition*, "the sixth sense" that we sometimes casually acknowledge, can help us if we choose to acknowledge and embrace its message. Intuition may be the only easily accessible representative guide that can release us from our illusions. When we pay attention to that intuition, a *new* set of choices may enable us to move from beyond this physical plane to the astral level and to a causal level and beyond—becoming and returning to what we always were—a part of God—as God. Many spiritual groups would term this phenomenon as *Christ Consciousness* or *Buddha Awareness*. This can occur for each of us, rather than to continue with the seemingly perpetual rounds of relative birth and death peppered with *relative good and relative evil.*

Because we chose our life path *before* we entered this life, our lives may seem to be predestined. That is only partially true because we have entered into a world that *we* have created. Thus, we have entered into an illusory creation—a fantasy world of our own making. Our lives and all that occurs within its relative confines are truly illusionary. They don't really exist.

I certainly acknowledge how that may seem to be a logical impossibility. But we are not dealing with logic, we are dealing with Spirit.

I am reminded of an episode from the TV series, *Star Trek*. Captain Picard and his crew of the *Starship Enterprise* often took a *holiday* from the stresses of their seemingly never-ending mission to explore the universe and beyond by way of a *holodeck*. The holodeck was a device that allowed the crew to "travel" through time, space, and circumstances and enter an existence that they created for their vacation. As a crew member entered the holodeck, they entered into an illusionary world which they desired and created. Their creations were *vacations from reality* where they could recharge themselves with a new and different life experience.

In this holodeck experience, each would live the life they created and would return to the Enterprise at a pre-selected ending time. Of course, they knew it was an illusion. However, during the experience they didn't fully realize that the experience was an illusion and were able to enjoy or despair the relative experiences. Yes, of course, this was a television story written by human fiction writers. But does that *Star Trek* experience mimic our own life as we know it?

We are dealing with the quantum world. The real *you* is the soul-being that resides in that space between and beyond, that mysterious and illusive *other* world. Indeed, if we are not thinking with Love, because only Love is real and the ticket to your spiritual growth, then we are living in an illusionary world or, as some would say, truly not thinking at all. Are we choosing to live in the world of relative evil? If so, we are choosing to live in our own created *hell*. Or, are we choosing to live in a world of relative good? If so, we are choosing to live in *heaven* on earth.

Consequently, good and evil, are only present on this plane of existence. It was a chosen act for each of us playing in concert with a cast of innumerable co-creators both in our pre-lives and in the physical realm. Good and evil, therefore, really don't exist at all. Good and evil are choices we as individuals and groups have made in our pre-lives so as to learn the lessons in order to ascend to higher spiritual levels and to eventually leave the wheel of birth and death and live in the infinite, not the relative physical creation.

And make no mistake about it, every thought we have, every decision we make is a CHOICE. The choices we make each moment determine how our lives unfold, our relationships, our abundance and our future, both in this world and beyond.

The suggestion that life is an illusion is, for most of us, a difficult concept to grasp. Death, however, is simply the end of the grand illusion. Death cannot be and is not the media created menacing image of the grim reaper draped in black with a skeletal face and carrying a frightening scythe, a common illusion. Death is merely a transition, from finite to infinite, a completion of yet another journey. If one needs to return to a corporeal existence, it will be because one has not completed the contract with one's soul—one's purpose in life. One may choose to return to a world similar to this one with a renewed contract of re-learning. One may also continue to choose a birth-death cycle until one has learned the lesson created in the pre-life and fulfilled that purpose in this life. We will continue this re-learning until we find the path to and the realization of our Source, God.

We must continue to realize and embrace the fact that, *we are not, as we often choose to believe, primarily a body with a soul, but a soul that is currently visiting in a body.*

Our world is a relative world. There is up and down, hot and cold, good and evil and so on. Good and evil are relative terms and acts because our world is a relative world—an illusionary world. Because this is so, good and evil cannot truly exist, except in the illusion we create in our created world. When the body dies, the entire illusion dies. Is it death as we think it to be? Perhaps or perhaps not. Yet we must remember that the illusion never really existed. The world we created never truly existed. Good and evil never existed. The pain and suffering we seem to witness never existed. It is not because God doesn't exist, it's because our physical life doesn't truly exist.

All we have is the NOW. There is no past, it is over and there is no future because the future is still an illusion yet to be created. In fact, there is no pain and suffering, only an illusion of such that we ourselves have created. God does exist, but not as the white-bearded figure we have created in our minds and folklore. He exists within us. He is the voice inside. He is us. Our ego is our most formidable enemy, always opting for its own preservation. Remember again, the old newspaper comic strip called Pogo and the anthropomorphic star Opossum in the strip. His common admonition was, "We have met the enemy—and he is us."—Such a profound statement from a 'possum!'

We do not have to be the enemy or be claimed by the fractious ego. We can *choose* to rise above our lower self and return to be the God-being that we are. We must, however, actively *choose* to do that.

Works Cited

1. Coddington, Robert H., *Death Brings Many Surprises*, pp. 130–132. Coddington delineates several reasons why it is not in our best interest to remember our past karmic involvements.

    a) In the matter of karmic debt, perceived as having been incurred by a past-life offense against one whose Spirit may now be incarnate in someone of your present acquaintance, you may consciously strive to make restitution out of fear of his reprisal. Conversely, if the past-life offense was against "you," you may be motivated by resentment to seek retaliation against the perpetrator's present life counterpart. Neither fear of reprisal nor desire to retaliate is conducive to raising your consciousness in this life.

b) Another individual may be obligated to you for a past-life favor. Given knowledge of this, you might be tempted to consciously seek return of that favor, the expectation of reward influencing your attitudes and actions—and distorting your values and decisions.

c) Some persons misperceive the fruits of Karma as the fabric of predestination and simply resign themselves to "fate." This attitude is fatal to the very concept of free will.

d) Foreknowledge of the identities of those you are to meet again, and of your past-life relationships to them, can lead to inappropriate overtures. For example, knowledge that one newly encountered in this life was your lover in another incarnation certainly will color your interaction with that person today. We are charged with responding to others as they *are,* not as they were as some other mortal.

e) Awareness of Karma and reincarnation can cause some persons to procrastinate in their development, much as once the case with the Spirits before physical man. Why, one may reason, should I strive in this lifetime for edification when there appears to be an eternity of lifetimes? This may contribute to a philosophy of "enjoy now, pay later," extended over a cosmic time frame. This is not the way to enlightenment.

f) The concept of Karma is used by some as a cop-out. Every minor reversal of fortune, every slight affliction, and every error of judgment is attributed to karmic harassment—perceived as a form of karmic punishment for past misdeeds. These individuals seem to believe that they would never make a mistake—make a wrong decision, trip over a rug, or catch a cold, if it weren't for their respective Spirit's continual imposition of petty karmic punishments. This attitude does little to encourage such persons to sharpen their judgment, develop agility, or mind their physical resistance to disease—but then why should it, when in their eyes they already would be perfect but for Karma.

CHAPTER 12

WHAT IS THE POWER OF INTENTION & LAW OF ATTRACTION?

ONE OF THE basic accepted laws of physics is the Newtonian concept that "for every action there is an opposite and equal reaction." This universal physical law has stood well over time when dealing with macro-physics on which most science is based. It is no less true, however, when dealing in the spiritual realm. We, who are trying to make sense of the world, have accepted that law and have labeled it the Law of Cause and Effect. Hindus call it the Law of Karma. The law teaches us that science doesn't have a lock on or ownership of the term. We also see it in many spiritual readings passed down through generations in the form of what is termed, The Golden Rule. Ah, if we could all only live by its dictates, we might all reach our spiritual goals enmass. "Do unto others as you would have others do unto you" is a wonderful and poignant axiom that points the way on the highway to heaven for each of us. It requires, however, the activation of one's power of intention. We need to know what intention is and how can we activate it.

There is a common dictionary definition of intent or intention. Namely; *"A strong purpose or aim, accompanied by a determination to produce a desired result."* There is really much more to this understanding of intention than such a definition. Let's look at a more spiritual approach:

> *Intent is a force that exists in the universe. When sorcerers (those who live of the Source) beckon intent, it comes to them and sets up the path for attainment, which means that sorcerers always accomplish what they set out to do.* [1]

Carlos Castaneda, spiritual teacher, author of several books featuring the teachings of Don Juan, used these words to describe the actual root of intention. He went on to say the following:

> *In the universe there is an immeasurable, indescribable force which shamans call intent, and absolutely everything that exists in the entire cosmos is attached to intent by a connecting link.* [2]

Can you fathom that! Intent is not something you do, but rather a force that exists in the universe as an invisible field of energy! Who knew? Can we all be sorcerers as Castaneda suggests? Can we all tap into that invisible intent that is ours to choose? What is needed is for us to pay attention to our thoughts and feelings as they emanate from the mind and subconscious and subsequently present us with choices. Yes, once again, choice. Life proceeds according to our intention for it. You choose your life. The intentions we choose direct the flow of our energy, and life, of course, is simply energy. What we think, we create, and what we create attracts more of the same. So the trick is to *pay attention to our intentions!*

William James, psychologist, who lived from 1842–1910 said,

> *There is a law in psychology that if you form a picture in your mind of what you would like to be, and you keep and hold that picture there long enough, you will soon become exactly as you have been thinking.*

Each moment our lives are bombarded with seemingly random thoughts that enter our brains in a multifaceted emotional shower that appear almost chaotic. Innumerable bits of observation and input dealing with emotions and feelings crash into our lives, confusing our thoughts, and challenging our intentions, making it almost impossible to sort them out into any thoughtful order and reason. However, this showering of thought and feelings in our minds can be viewed as opportunities to focus our intent. If we have the desire and ability to ponder a thought, we can change it, and change our lives accordingly. Moment to moment we are given the opportunity to create a new thought and a new intent. As we change our desires, our intent, we change how we think. When the way we think changes, we take a new direction on a road that leads us to a new path. It is then that the *will* takes over.

We must, however, first *intend* to do so. Intent is in our grasp. It is up to us to choose our thoughts, emotions, and feelings. We have always had that capacity and now we have the opportunity and need to act upon it. Often, we look closely at thoughts that ask questions such as, *Why does this always seem to happen to me?* In truth it doesn't just happen to you. You chose it. The path away from such a dilemma is to take command of your intent and *choose* your thoughts. We tend to allow ourselves to become the victims of our own false and fearful thoughts and feelings. We must learn to live in positive thoughts and feelings of our own making. *We get to do that!*

We are creatures who are endowed with the power of intention. We can co-create our lives with our positive thoughts by paying close attention to what we are intending and attracting with our thoughts. When we live our lives with thoughts and feeling that we intend, we have the ultimate power over ourselves. We are living with intention. From this point, the *Law of Attraction*[3] takes over.

A Course in Miracles says the following:

> *The source of all our experience is mind. The true nature of mind is limitless transcendent awareness and creative power. However, our mistaken thoughts and beliefs, which directs the mind's activity, appear to distort, constrict, and fragment it. Consequently, we must change our thoughts and beliefs in order to correct our perception and restore the mind to its full potential.*

The Law of Attraction received a boost in publicity with the literary publication and subsequent movie, *The Secret*. For those who haven't experienced either of these presentations, suffice to say that they quickly became "cult classics." There is no doubt this universal law of attraction exists and is operative from consciousness and from intention. The book and movie, however, seemed to suggest the basic premise that the purpose of the law applies primarily to the material world—that is, attaining material wealth and possessions. Yes, it also talks some about perfect health attainment and dabbles in quantum physics from some very impressive physicists, spiritual guides, and folks who are metaphysical students and teachers. It focuses, however, on attracting temporary wealth—the kind of *wealth* you will leave on this plane of existence when your body transcends to another plane. You know the drill by now, think about what you want, perseverate on it, live as though you have it or are it, and it will become reality. There is no doubt that if one were to exercise that kind of desire and intention, those material benefits could surely come to you. Indeed, I can attest to that in my own personal life.

But it is curious to me why *The Secret* emphasizes attracting material objects rather than spiritual awareness. Where is the emphasis on attracting spiritual understanding, attracting love and dismissing fear? If one were to extrapolate the benefits of the law of attraction as espoused by *The Secret*, one might assume that the path of the soul ran through an upscale European Car Dealer. Perhaps in *The Secret's* analysis, the bumper sticker philosophy *"He who has the most toys, wins,"* would be the chief operating principle. That's fine if that is the only race you choose to enter. *You get to do that!*

But there is a much more meaningful pursuit of our existence here on earth. When we look inside and give serious attention and intent to why we are here or what we might best be doing while we're here, then the law of attraction takes on a much deeper and meaningful role. It becomes the pursuit of life transcending to the next level of *living*. Most of the world's inhabitants choose to call it death, but let's not panic in the face of what others may think. Our whole concept of death is often misstated and misunderstood in this world. Only when we journey inside do we see and understand that death is but another waystation of life, a stopover in our journey in connecting with our soul—not the frightful fear of a hellish, burning hole guarded by a shadowy figure known as the Grim Reaper.

I give some credit to *The Secret*, however. It, indeed, produced a conversation on the law of attraction and opened those new thoughts in the minds of many. Those who pay attention to the law will benefit in ways they only dreamed. I also give credit and thanks to such luminaries as Oprah Winfrey, as well as many celebrity promoters for fostering the beginning of *essential conversations* and bringing spiritual awareness to the general population through the power of celebrity and the mass media. That kind of awareness can only help our world seek to raise our collective vibration to the *Oneness* we are. For we as humans to understand that the laws and the universe are not random activities, and that thought can produce wonders, especially if the thought is commonplace amongst a population, is a cosmic wonder in and of itself. The more we understand the power of our minds, the power of intention, and the law of attraction and how our attitudes and destinies can be mitigated and controlled by our perceptions or ourselves and our situations, the more we understand how to live.

Now is the time of awakening—for us all to be aware of the power of intention and the law of attraction. Without such knowledge and awareness we will continue to stay embroiled in physical and mental suffering and not have the capacity to approach the superconsciousness that leads us back to our Oneness with our Source.

WORKS CITED

1. Castanada, Carlos, *The Active Side of Infinity*, pg. 10
2. Castanada, Carlos, Ibid. pg.10.
3. The attractive, magnetic power of the universe that draws similar energies together. It manifests through the power of creation, everywhere and in multiple ways. It manifests through your thoughts by drawing to you thoughts and ideas of a similar kind. It is the law of power that brings together people of similar interests and unites them into special groups.

CHAPTER 13

HOW DO AFFIRMATIONS HELP US?

An affirmation can give strength to an idea or request that you are holding in your heart, thus accelerating your readiness for its arrival in your life.

—*Annie Elizabeth[1]*

ERHAPS ONE OF the most useful tools in training and disciplining one's mind and thoughts is affirming to the brain the direction you wish it to follow while pursuing your spiritual path through Love and Joy. A companion tool in the pursuit of spirituality, along with prayer and meditation, affirmations contain the power of the spoken word and help to align one's intent with one's creative manifestation.

Paramahansa Yogananda describes such power.

Infinite potencies of sound derive from the creative word. Any word spoken with clear realization and deep concentration has a materializing value. Words saturated with sincerity, conviction, faith, and intuition are like highly explosive vibration bombs, which, when set off, shatter the rocks of difficulties and create the change desired.[2]

The use of an affirmation can direct your mind to have new thoughts. Given the intense thought conditioning that comprises who you have come to believe you are, through the use of affirmations your mind is refreshed, your thoughts change and you wake up to your true self, if only temporarily. The affirmation invites your mind to travel along a new line of thinking, which it actually finds exciting and exhilarating—that is, until the new thought butts up against something that threatens the ego's comfortable position of authority. So expect your affirmations to stir things up for you. If you feel upset, it's an invitation to explore more deeply the thoughts going through your mind and gain an understanding of that which is causing the disturbance. When you react to an experience or a thought you are having, your mental state produces energy that attracts more thoughts and consequently more experiences of a similar vibration or frequency. That is, negative thoughts attract negative experiences. Affirmations support you in responding to your experiences in a way that allows you to move to a level of better feeling and a more positive energy vibration. Over time, you retrain your mind to choose this better feeling rather than continually being drawn into drama and unhappiness.

Through the use of affirmations, we become more able to recognize and undo destructive or harmful thoughts. Affirmations create a more positive interpretation and response to our world, thereby increasing our experience of contentment, peace, and joy

As depicted by the earlier quote, Paramahansa Yogananda was a strong proponent of affirmations. It was his belief that an affirmation, if strong and conscious enough, can react on the body and mind through the subconscious. He goes on to say that the stronger affirmations reach not only the subconscious, but also to what we have referred to as the superconscious mind—the major storehouse of miraculous powers.

Most teachers recommend that affirmations follow some conscious steps to fully access the power of the practice. Generally, those conscious steps include the following:

- Turn inward into silence for an appointed time of your choosing for 5 or 10 minutes.

- Observe your state of mind and feelings that are present in your body.

- Ask yourself, what would I like to be, do, or have more of, in my life today?

- When you have targeted a goal for the day, or a disturbing thought that you wish to clear, write or locate an affirmation to work on.

- After choosing an affirmation, repeat the entire thought to yourself.

- Repeat it again loudly, then slowly, and then gradually more slowly until your voice is beyond a whisper.

- Gradually affirm the thought without moving your tongue or lips until you have a reached a continuity of uninterrupted thought.

- Be patient and attentive as profound repetitions become miracle workers.

- Continuing affirmations beyond these points will bring you an increasing sense of joy and peace.

All affirmation teachers caution us not to blindly follow an affirmation or prayer with meaningless repetition. As in prayer, one does not become a thoughtless, non-sincere praying machine, but should always strive to invoke sincerity and desire in our affirming thoughts.

Finally, remember that affirmations are simply interactions with energy. Inasmuch as we are all energy beings and we create our world through our thoughts, we have control over what we create. Indeed, we are what we think.

Works Cited

1.   Annie Elizabeth, *Affirmations for Everyday Living*, pg.2 (For a wonderful treatise on affirmations loaded with examples and process, see this gift of inspiration.)

2.   Yogananda, Paramahansa, *Where There is Light*, pgs. 28–29.

CHAPTER 14

WHAT IS THE WONDER OF QUANTUM PHYSICS?

W E TOUCHED A bit on quantum physics/mechanics in our discussion of "Who or What is God" and introduced some of the physicists who discovered the foundation of a new theory and proved its reality. It is such a misunderstood, hard to fathom, and mysterious phenomenon, that it is essential that it be examined in a bit more detail.

The thrust of quantum physics or quantum mechanics (it's really the same thing) is the real beginning of understanding of how everything in our universe comes to be. To understand the basics of quantum mechanics is our initial step in the unveiling of how science and spirit have moved so closely together in recent years.

From the initial experiments of Schrodinger and Heisenburg and the unraveling of parts of the mystery by Niels Bohr, physicists have discovered new laws in the working of the clockwork universe. What we now should be calling them is *potentialities,* rather than fixed laws, but we are still learning the rudiments of the whole quantum process. *Potentiality implies that an assumption could happen, yet your thoughts could alter the result depending on your perceptions. (WOW!)*

The benefits of learning about quantum mechanics allows us to more fully understand why faith, positive thinking, and personal actions, can actually change one's consciousness and circumstances to allow the power you never truly knew or could prove you have. It teaches us that the entire universe is fully connected and exists as one entity composed of an infinite number of parts, including us. As the book title implies, There's Only One of us Here! Quantum mechanics shows we have been perpetuating the illusion that we are all separate while demonstrating that mind and matter interact and connect. It shows how we can be co-creators with God, and most amazingly, that it is relatively easy to create your life and its outcomes.

To begin our simple understanding of quantum physics, let's look at some basic known scientific assumptions. Most of us know or understand through our study of biology that the body is made of cells. The cells, we are taught, are made up of molecules—which are made up of atoms. So far, so good, Huh?

Atoms, in turn, are made up of sub-atomic particles known as electrons, protons and neutrons. Your body, the plants around us, the animals, trees, rocks, water, and everything else in the physical world, including your vehicles, manufactured items, and dwellings, consist of these sub-atomic particles.

All of these sub-atomic particles are "packets of energy." These packets of energy are the *stuff* of the universe. Sub-atomic particles are not made up of energy, they *are* energy.

In other words, everything, and I mean everything, consists of the same stuff—molecules, atoms and space—the same composition of energy packets that comprises us. Can you imagine a rock or tree having the same composition of molecules, atoms and space that you do? I know. It's difficult.

Are you still with me? The only difference between you and the other physical objects and living things in your world is how these sub-atomic particles are grouped together into differing objects and how they vibrate. However, and here is where the discussion becomes even more phenomenal, a sub-atomic particle is not really a particle as you might equate with something like beach sand grains. Sub-atomic particles are not objects as we are taught to believe. They are, in fact, *probabilities* of existence. That is, they are more *potentiality* than objects. And, because they are potentiality, they can have *multiple* existences. That is, they can be two or more things at once—depending on how *you* choose to view them. They can be particle-like and wave-like at the same time. It all depends upon the observer. Yes, how YOU observe these particles influences whether they are particles or wave-like probabilities. This is why physicists initially were dumbfounded by their own discoveries.

Quantum physics is the study of how these waves and particles act and exactly what they are. We do know that they are "energy packets," pure energy. How these energy packets act is the marvel of quantum mechanics. They seem to arrange themselves into any object that we choose, simply by our observation and our will.

That is the mystery and seeming magic it presents. The whole reason they band together in a particular object is due to group or individual thoughts!

Wow! Is this a change in our perceptions of who and what we are? It is no wonder that physicist Schroedinger didn't want to believe it, at least not until Bohr convinced him of the reality of his own discovery. *What quantum mechanics shows is that we can deliberately, consciously, alone, or with groups, fashion our world with the power of thought!* Of course, there is much more to the study than I have outlined here and there is still much to learn. Quantum physics finds that when we observe the electron, the possibility of it being in two (or more) places at the same time becomes the actuality of being in one place momentarily while emitting a light and suddenly appearing in a different place *without traveling there*. This is known as a quantum leap. Imagine being where you are in this time and space and instantaneously being in another place at the same time without having to travel there or use time to get there! This might be termed the *speed of thought*, surpassing the speed of light! You can see why this has turned science upside down and rendered Newtonian physics as laws pertaining only to *large* objects moving relatively slowly—such as our observable physical world.

Newton was correct in his observances that physics is based on constants, depending on a measurable beginning point that doesn't vary or change. That's why the conclusions Newton developed were called laws. They were based on constants. He did remarkably scholarly work for his time and gave the world a primary understanding of how things should be that was honored for almost 400 years. However, modern studies can now measure the movements of large objects in minute degrees and has added a quantum analysis of classical physics. Newton was right for what evidence was available, but could not have the wherewithal to know that even large objects, such as the earth and entire universes are subject to potentiality by the understanding of quantum movement.

Dr. John Hagelin, who monikers himself as a Quantum Physicist and, parenthetically, one of the guest narrators on the popular movie, *The Secret*, actually put his quantum mechanical theory to work by raising over 90 million dollars and recruiting 4000 *trained full time meditators* to focus on how group thinking/meditating can change the course of the physical world. His experiment was designed to show how quantum physics defies the currently acceptable Newtonian physics and produce changes in the material world. He claimed that this action reduced the crime rate in Washington D.C. by 18%.[1] For those of you, like me, who are dropouts from the California Home for the Bewildered, when it gets too deep into theory, its time to take a closer look at the ramifications of these phenomena.

Quantum physics has proved:

a) That an object can be in two places at the same time

b) That the speed of light does not enter the equation when electrons in an atom change orbits without going there, and, because these atoms change orbit instantaneously—speed does not even enter into the discussion.

c) That in the final composition of any cell or molecule, living or not, there is only energy.

d) That the thoughts and actions of you, the observer, can change the outcome of how that energy is applied.

It is quite a change in perception to accept these points as the new reality. But that is exactly with what we must now contemplate, begin to accept, and contend. Welcome to the Quantum Age!

This change in the theory of physics and the acquisition of new discoveries and facts is a tremendous challenge to all of us. The facts as we know them have changed. Our world hasn't changed, but our perceptions on how the world works has now opened up our minds and has invited spirit and science to move vibrationally much closer. Indeed, there are a growing number of physicists, in the face of quantum mechanics, who now proclaim the death of science. Imagine such a proclamation! Is it any wonder that there is so much speculation about a shift in consciousness to be completed by the second decade of this (21st) century? Whether or not we can anticipate the death of science, we do know that quantum physics has introduced us to a new world enlightening us that the power of thought can change our perception and our world.

What an incredible opportunity and challenge we now face. Hello God! Hello Source! We are beginning the divine journey in the realization that we are all, indeed, One. *Hail to the new millennium!*

WORKS CITED

1.   Hagelin, John, www.*Wikipedia, The Free Encyclopedia*, (November, 2010)

CHAPTER 15

TODAY IS THE FIRST DAY OF THE REST OF YOUR LIFE

*"If you don't change directions,
you may end up where you are heading"*
—Lao Tzu

THERE IS A SHIFT taking place, a shift in consciousness. It is a miracle in action right before our eyes—all three of them. It actually began in earnest in 1987 when the world's consciousness shifted towards the Source, towards God. We labeled it the Harmonic Convergence, a vibrational energy shift caused by an unusual alignment of the planets in our solar system. Many of our brethren ignored this phenomenon believing it to be a conversation only worthy of crazy folks who somehow thought the universal clockwork was not random and chaotic. Quantum physics has helped to bridge that gap in understanding even as the bulk of the world still chooses to ignore what is happening.

Dr. David Hawkins, a noted and respected spiritual teacher and scientist, proclaimed that the vibrational level of the world crossed the 200 level in recent years[1] He stated that this vibrational level shift was a major key to the survival of the world as we know it. Such a shift meant that there are enough souls here that had risen above the necessary vibrational level to counterbalance those souls who are still much lower in vibration, reminding us again that we are all one. The shift was so subtle, that it seemed imperceptible—but not to those spirit beings who are present on this planet. The movement or shift in consciousness indicates a profound movement of consciousness by a host of beings moving inexorably towards the state of superconsciousness.

How does a shift in consciousness, seemingly imperceptible, manifest itself? Consider for a moment, the amoeba. You might remember that tiny little protoplasmic animal that we first heard about in our 7th grade science class? Do you recall how the amoeba moves? The amoeba is a simple and primitive animal and just a simple blob of protoplasmic material that has no limbs or visible means of moving or shifting from one spot to another. It moves by something biological scientists have labeled a *pseudopod,* or *false foot.* How does it move? A relatively significant bit of protoplasm, a vanguard of protoplasm directed by the animal itself, moves from the interior and extends the amoeba out in a direction eventually producing a mass movement within the little animal. The moving protoplasm produces a little *peninsula* that reshapes the amoeba. Slowly, but surely, and almost imperceptibly, the rest of the protoplasm also moves and eventually joins the *peninsula* until the entire mass has reformed in a different space. We do not know why it moves. It does move ever so slightly and slowly, and does, indeed, change position.

This is analogous to the shift in consciousness that the Harmonic Convergence initiated with the human race. A new thought form forms a new peninsula of consciousness and begins to draw the rest of the new thought towards it until it meshes as one. Such is the movement of our world's conscious thought. We have moved and are moving still. No, the thought consciousness has not completed the shift, but it is well under way. And yes, it may seem imperceptible, but we as a species are shifting our consciousness to a new place in this existence—truly a miracle.

You are part of God and God is part of you. In fact, we all are parts of God. We are all one. *There's only one of us here!* Impossible to comprehend? A cursory venture into quantum physics reveals a new understanding by science that, at the *sub-atomic level*, our *thoughts control matter.* We, and all the rocks, water, soil, flora and fauna, are simply molecules in various stages, propelled by those "packets of energy" to give us form through vibration and motion. All matter present in the universe is made of the same stuff. We all consist of the same kind of molecules, space and atoms that make up rocks, flora, fauna and the galaxy of stars and planets. We simply vibrate at a different rate which gives us the appearance of individual differences and behaviors. As we have come to understand this quantum principle, we know that all creation is made up of the same stuff and can be manipulated by our creative minds through focused spiritual thought to change the vibrations of the molecules. We are learning how to do that.

Because quantum mechanics has proved that thoughts can control matter, we can ascertain that there is more here than simple blind faith and what our five senses have revealed to us.

Our venerable Albert Einstein, one who we ascribe as perhaps our most brilliant physicist, who at first denied the precepts of quantum physics, has declared this to be true. Einstein said,

> *The distinction between past, present and future is only an illusion, however persistent.*

We, in our corporeal lives, are governed by five senses. What we see, hear, smell, taste and touch reflects and indicates our limited truth, our limited reality. This limitation is constantly reinforced by our self-perpetuating ego. The common perpetuation of negative world news and fearful information from those in power, down to our immediate personal circle, is exploiting our fear based on what we have and can experience, using and limited to only our five senses. Our thoughts seem to us to be as random as our lives are full of seemingly random and chaotic acts and events. But in truth what we desire, what we focus upon, what we truly direct our minds towards, will ultimately be manifested. That manifestation, in turn, will assuredly come to us in the form of good or evil, love or fear.

We may not immediately notice these manifestations, because time itself is relative to our corporeal existence—yet they come to past. After all, we are creating these manifestations, together, and with our thoughts.

We don't generally choose to grasp the forces and power of our spiritual nature. Most of us don't choose to complicate our lives with new thinking that challenges that with which we are comfortable. However, those forces are part of our whole being and have the power to create exactly what we desire. Accordingly, when we don't focus our thoughts and desires, the apparent random and chaotic events that surround us tend to govern our lives. Those random thoughts and events direct us and we are reacting instead of acting.

And when we are without a purpose, a plan, a pathway—one that we are certainly capable of producing—we continually traverse the circle of birth and death with both good and bad things happening in our life.

Too few choose a path to enlightenment—the path of Love and Joy. We have *forgotten* that we *always* attract that which our thoughts create. This is a prime example of the *Law of Attraction*, discussed earlier in this book. Any applicable rule that our common human law commands is that we tend to obey it. It doesn't ask us to believe in any law, just obey it—and if you choose to not obey—you do so at your own risk and bear the common law consequences.

But one can change common law if one chooses and with the cooperation of one's society. Conversely, the rule of God's Law is that you don't have to believe in him. God just is. You can choose to know him or not. No, God isn't that stereotypical man-made visual creation that sits on a throne in some astral and heavenly atmosphere with angels flying around playing harps. God simply **is** as in ourselves and what we create. Your choice dictates your future.

So, in honor of the new millennium of spiritual pursuit, I present the following, a verse from *A Course in Miracles*. It expresses so well the reality of spirit and the powerlessness of illusion.

Spirit is in a state of grace forever.
Your reality is only spirit.
Therefore you are in a state of grace forever.
Spirit makes us of mind
As means to find its Self-expression.
And the mind which serves the spirit
Is at peace and filled with joy...

Yet mind can also see itself
Divorced from spirit,
And perceive itself within a body
It confuses with itself.
Without its function
Then it has no peace,
And happiness is alien to its thoughts.
Your mind can be possessed by illusions,
But spirit is eternally free.
And so it goes...

WORKS CITED

1. Hawkins, David, *Power vs. Force.* pg. 6. Hawkins refers to a relatively new (1971) process of behavioral kinesiology wherein he expands on Dr. John Diamond's startling discovery that indicator muscles would strengthen and weaken in the presence of positive or negative emotional, intellectual, and physical stimuli. Hawkins researched and developed a means of calibrating a scale of relative truth on a scale from 1 to 1,000. Two hundred indicated that mankind has reached a new threshold of profound consciousness.

ANNOTATED REFERENCES

1. Berg, Yehuda (2001). *The Powers of Kabbalah*. San Diego, California: Jodere Group.

    The ancient mysteries of the Kabbalah are chronicled and explained by one of the living masters of Jewish mysticism. Berg suggests that 99% of our being is "on the other side of the curtain" while just 1% is represented by our corporeal lives. He explains the ancient symbols and leads the reader on a fascinating journey into the alchemic mysteries of life.

2. Butler-Bowden, Tom. (2005) *50 Spiritual Classics*. London, UK: Nicholas Brealey Publishing.

    Butler-Bowden presents us with overviews of 50 spiritual scholars and leaders in this well-researched body of work. If you want a thumb-nail sketch of a wide variety of spiritual leaders, pick up this book. It will become your initial sojourn into the study of 50 classical spiritual leaders.

3. Capra, Fritjof (1976). *The Tao of Physics*. Boulder, Colorado: Shambhala Publications by arrangement with Bantam Books.

    This is a "wow" book. Capra adeptly takes us on a journey melding science with Western & Eastern spiritual thought. He explains the rudiments of the major religions while comparing them to today's science. His conclusions, backed by incredible knowledge of spiritual thought, religion, and physics, gives the reader a feeling of how and why our science and spirituality merge.

4. Carey, Ken (1991). *The Third Millennium*. New York: HarperCollins.

    Another book that is a true gift for all *Lightseekers!* Carey talks about the end of history as we know it as we move to a new era of consciousness. This book is a wonderful read, prophetic and gives an explanation of how and when the new era will present itself and the ways we can prepare ourselves.

5. Castaneda, Carlos (1998). *The Active Side of Infinity.* New York: Harper Collins.

    More of the teachings of Don Juan. A classic book that takes us through what Castaneda has learned from his incredible spiritual journey with Don Juan as his teacher. This book reads as an autobiographical novel that focuses on the spiritual development and challenges of the student while both teacher and student are bonded together by destiny.

6. Chaney, Earlyne & Robert (2008). *Astara's Book of Life*, Rancho Cucamonga, California: Astara.

    The founders of Astara began in 1951 to create "The Mystery School" which today boasts thousands of members worldwide. The organization today operates as a membership group dedicated to the writings and revelations of Earlyne & Robert. Astara considers itself a church for all religions knowing that all paths lead to the summit. Primarily based on a mystical Christian viewpoint, yet acknowledging that they are one of the paths, not the only path. *The Book of Life*, an initial gift from the organization for membership is a series of lessons for the spiritual seeker that begins with the very basics without insulting your intelligence or path. For example, there is a lesson on meditation that is well explained and easy to adjust. You can reach them at *www. astara.org.*

7. Chopra, Deepak (2004). *The Book of Secrets: Unlocking the Hidden Dimensions of your Life.* New York: Three Rivers Press.

    We all want to find a soul mate, perhaps a new career or how to teach our children well. As we look for personal breakthroughs, here is Deepak Chopra who once again comes to our aid. He presents the fifteen secrets that can change your life. They include the secrets of perfect love, healing, compassion, and faith. He points out that the greatest hunger in life is not for food, money, success, status, security, sex, or even love from the opposite sex. The deepest hunger in life is a secret that only is revealed when a person is willing to unlock a hidden part of the self. He teaches us how to do that.

8. Chopra, Deepak (date). *The Spontaneous Fulfillment of Desire.*

    One of Chopra's highly interesting books on potential and destiny. A NY Times best seller, this book takes a close look at *coincidence* and the relative conspiring of unforeseen events in our lives. Chopra comments on the concept of *synchronicity,* the reality of miracles.

9. Chopra, Deepak (1994). *The Seven Spiritual Laws of Success: A Practical Guide to the Fulfillment of Your Dreams.* San Rafael, California: Amber-Allen/New World Library.

> Chopra takes you through the fundamentals of spirituality through seven common spiritual laws while outlining and suggesting actual exercises to allow you to understand and practice the way to enlightenment. Each chapter is short and to the point. A great read.

10. Coddington, Robert H. (1987). *Death Brings Many Surprises, A Psychic Handbook.* New York: Ballantine Books/Random House.

> A nice handbook of the psychic world that is well written, simple to understand with language that doesn't frighten folks away. The author discusses how reality isn't real, the number of minds we access, the interplay of spirits, reincarnation, transitions, the paranormal and what to do now. His discussion on why we don't remember our past lives is astute and explicit.

11. Cota-Robles, Patricia Diane (1997). *What on Earth is Going On?* Tucson, Arizona: New Age Study of Humanity's Purpose, Inc.

> A metaphysical journey into the vibrational shift that is occurring on earth at this moment. Cota-Robles has dedicated her life to understanding and communicating with the spiritual path of our civilization as well as tuning into our place and role in the universe. Earth has been a minor player seeking a new dimensional shift that is now taking place in this early 21st century. This book takes us on a new journey beyond the 3rd dimension and vaults us towards the 5th dimension because of the increased vibrational movement that is taking place.

12. DeVries, Ardeth (2010) *The Space Between.* Felton, California: River Sanctuary Publishing.

> A wonderful and wistful romp in that space between incarnations of physical lives. DeVries introduces us to many spiritual characters along the way that represent issues that we all face in our lives. A fun, informative and delightful book that will bring a smile to the reader while teaching valuable lessons about ourselves. In truth, DeVries writes her own spiritual autobiography.

13. Dossey, Dr. Larry (1999). *Reinventing Medicine: Beyond Mind-Body to a New Era of Healing.* San Francisco: HarperCollins.

> Dr. Dossey documents his work and demonstrates that we can use our

mind, enlist prayer, and "non-local" healing to change the parameters of working with healing. Referring to double-blind studies, Dossey documents the power of prayer in healing. Here is a chance for the reader to observe the studies that lead to these remarkable conclusions and open the path that coincides with his medical expertise. Prepare for a sojourn into non-physical healing that opens new and exciting horizons for healing.

14. Dyer, Dr. Wayne (2004). *The Power of Intention: Learning to Co-Create Your world Your Way.* Carlsbad, California: Hay House.

This work is so easy to understand with the passionate guidance of Dr. Wayne Dyer. If one wishes to understand the rudiments of what the power of intention is, and how it can be harnessed, this is the book for you.

15. Dyer, Dr. Wayne (1998). *Wisdom of the Ages: 60 Days to Enlightenment,* New York: HarperCollins

Another jewel by Dr. Dyer. This book is Dyer's research on a host of spiritual teachers, each bringing light to a new genre of thought, meditation, prayer and a myriad of other spiritual values. After each essay, Dyer provides exercises for the reader to work on as a result of the lessons by the masters. If you want to know the essence of spiritual masters such as Lao Tzu, Buddha, Cicero, Jesus, St. Francis, Rumi and 60 others, get this book.

16. Dyer, Dr. Wayne (2007). *Change Your Thoughts—Change Your Life: Living the Wisdom of the Tao.* Carlsbad, California: Hay House.

Another masterpiece by Dr. Dyer. Here he takes the writing of the Tao and extrapolates the ancient teachings and relates them to how we can utilize and live this gentle, ancient wisdom. A wondrous read—you need not read it starting from page one, but have pleasure dipping into the wisdom simply by opening to any page.

17. Eden, Donna (1988). *Energy Medicine.* New York: Tarcher/Putnam.

An energy healer of the first magnitude, Eden shows you how to use your body's energy to heal yourself and keep yourself physically and spiritually healthy. She uses clairvoyant observations of energy patterns that have led to a practical guide to manage the body's energy.

18. Elizabeth, Annie (2010). *Affirmations for Everyday Living: Create more clarity, success and joy in your daily life.* Felton, California: River Sanctuary Publishing.

What a treasure! Each practical affirmation gives the reader avenues of personal healing and recovery by introducing everyday situations that we all face. Annie Elizabeth gives us the process of developing our own affirmations and shows us how her personal journey allowed her to develop this special work over her lifetime.

19. Foundation for Inner Peace. (1975 -1985). *A Course in Miracles*, Tiburon, California: Foundation for Inner Peace.

> The basic inspired text of New Thought. It truly is a "course" offering daily lessons in spirituality. It is not a book that you read as a novel or another lightly considered reading. It starts out by saying, "This is a course in miracles. It is a required course." With that prepare yourself for a lifetime of reference and promise and guidance.

20. Gibran, Kahlil (1962). *The Prophet*. New York: Alfred A. Knopf.

> Perhaps the most inspiring set of prose written this past century. Gibran talks about a myriad of personal subjects that touch all who experience his spiritual connection with his subjects. *This book is a must read for everyone!*

21. Goswami, Amit (2000). *The Visionary Window: A Quantum Physicist's Guide to Enlightenment*. Wheaton, Illinois: The Theosophical Publishing House.

> If one truly wants to understand the relationship between spirituality and physics, this is the source for your answers to those complex ideas. Goswami instructs us on how quantum physics has turned the once sacred "laws" of Issac Newton on its head when applied to atomic theory.

22. Greaves, Helen (1969) *Testimony of Light*. New York: Penguin Group.

> Frances Banks passed on and communicated with her best friend and colleague, Helen Greaves, from the next world. Helen records the remarkable dictations from Frances as she chronicles the "life" she finds in the next plane of existence. Truly a fascinating discussion of what life after death brings for us.

23. Harvey, Andrew (2000). *The Direct Path, Creating a Personal Journey to the Divine Using the World's Spiritual Traditions*. New York: Broadway Books, a division of Random House.

> Harvey is the co-author/editor of the classic and bestselling *The Tibetan Book of Living and Dying*. Go with him as he leads you directly to the

heart of the matter, the source, and the spirit of all life. He creates an illuminating spiritual map that anyone can use to develop a direct path to the divine without relying on churches, gurus, or other intermediaries

24. Hawkins, David R. (2002). *Power Vs. Force: The Hidden Determinates of Human Behavior.* Carlsbad, California: Hay House.

A powerful book on diagnosis and healing through muscle testing. Hawkins has documented his work with thousands of subjects and has classified them with a spiritually descriptive number range that indicates where they are in their spiritual quest by simple kinesthetic testing that anyone can do. Follow this book up with *the Eye of the I* and the final book of the trilogy, *I.*

25. Hay, Louise L. (1984) *You Can Heal Your Life.* Santa Monica, California: Hay House, Inc.

A book that defines our problems, examines where they come from, whether the problem is true and what to do now. Chock full of exciting information that explains her beliefs and the basis for her teaching. Hay has her own publishing company that has risen to the top of spirituality related books. Another great read.

26. Hicks, Esther and Jerry Hicks. (The Teachings of Abraham). (2004) *Ask and it Is Given: Learning to Manifest Your Desires.* Carlsbad, California: Hay House.

This is an excellent book that deals with the Law of Attraction. It is well written, easy to follow with dozens of suggestions on how our intentions govern our attractions. Highly recommended.

27. Hicks, Esther and Jerry Hicks, (The Teaching of Abraham). (2006*). The Amazing Power of Deliberate Intent: Living the Art of Allowing.* Carlsbad, California: Hay House.

What is your deliberate intent? Presenting the teachings of the non-physical entity, Abraham, Esther & Jerry Hicks assist in noting that awareness is needed to balance your energy and to live the Art of Allowing along the way. As such, you'll find that the living of your life is an ongoing journey of joy, rather than a series of long dry spells between occasional moments of temporary satisfaction. This is a great follow-up to their previous book, *Ask and it Is Given.*

28. Holmes, Ernest (1938: 1998). *The Science of Mind: A Philosophy, a Faith, a Way of Life*. New York: Tarcher/Putnam.

> Written by the founder of Religious Science, this book is the "bible" for practitioners of New Thought. Nearly 700 pages long, Holmes' philosophy is outlined and meticulously explained including the nature of being, spiritual mind healing, spiritual mind healing practices, and what he terms "the perfect whole." An exquisitely valuable resource that is a must for your bookshelf.

29. Jampolsky, Dr. Gerald G. (1979). *Love is Letting Go of Fear*. Berkeley, California: Celestial Arts.

> One of the first books from an author who was intrinsically involved after the original development of *A Course in Miracles*. A short, easy to read and understand book that introduces without complications, the choices between Love and fear.

30. Kardec, Allan (2003). *The Gospel: Explained by the Spiritist Doctrine*. Philadelphia, Pennsylvania: Alan Kardec Educational Society.

> There is a considerable following for Kardec's work…and several books that talk about the Spiritist Doctrine. This book follows the bible and interprets it from an enlightened Spiritist perspective rather than from beliefs that have fed Christian doctrine for centuries. Highly interesting, especially for those who know something about the Bible.

31. Katie, Byron (2002). *Loving What Is: Four Questions That Can Change Your Life*. New York: Three Rivers Press.

> Also known as "The Work." This is a practical book that so wonderfully shows us how to work with the realities of life through four thoughtful and practical questions of yourself. Surprisingly simple, yet so incredibly effective! Katie, as she is called, conducts workshops all over the world using her methods. *Pick this book up as soon as possible!* You will be thrilled at her insights and practical methodologies from someone who has lived through and beyond powerlessness.

32. Kornfield, Jack (2001) *After the Ecstasy, The Laundry; How the Heart Grows Wise on the Spiritual Path*. New York: Bantam Books.

> Written by a modern day Buddhist, Kornfield reminds us to pursue the spiritual, but also to do the "laundry"…i.e. pay attention to what you are doing in this realm. Highly readable, incredibly incisive, and

a wonderful lesson from someone who has spent his life in spiritual pursuits.

33. Krishnamurti, J. (1991) *Meeting Life*, New York: HarperCollins

Once chosen by The Theosophical Society to become the next world spiritual leader, Krishnamurti did not want to participate in a structured spiritual leadership role. Instead, he traveled the world and became one of the most trusted independent spiritual guides ever to touch the West. His talks and writings in this book focus upon finding your path without retreating from society.

34. Krishnamurti, J. (1980) *Truth and Actuality.* San Francisco: Harper & Row.

An excellent introduction for those who haven't yet experienced J. Krishnamurti. It begins with a mind-stretching discussion between Krishnamurti and renowned theoretical physicist, David Boem. His talks and dialogues considers how one's consciousness is filled with misconceptions about the self, what those misconceptions are, and how to transcend them.

35. Lake, Gina (2008) *Embracing the Now.* Sedona, Arizona: Endless Satsang Foundation.

The true source of happiness is the Now—this moment. A very clear and precise treatise of essays and practices to assist us in understanding the power of the Now and what we can do to achieve such a state. Wonderful insights and wisdom dominate this book. Another book we used in our spirituality seminars that garnered much praise and use by our participants.

36. Lipton, Bruce (2005). *The Biology of Belief: Unleashing the Power of Consciousness, Matter and Miracles.* Santa Rosa, California: Mountain of Love/Elite Books.

This is an amazing book. Lipton, an MD, medical school professor, and energetic scientist, has a wonderful explanation of how we control our cellular biology. With an ample dash of quantum physics, he gives us a layman's romp showing how medical science is changing due to the new facts revealed by quantum physics.

37. Long, Jeffrey, MD (2010) *Evidence of the Afterlife, The Science of Near-Death Experiences.* New York: Harpercollins.

Is there life after death? Dr. Long has examined hundreds of documentations of near-death experiences and provides compelling evidence that mind and consciousness cannot be reduced to brain activity. Long's research will facilitate opening your mind to the realization that there is no such thing as death.

38. McTaggert, Lynn (2002). *The Field: The Quest for the Secret Force of the Universe*. New York: HarperCollins.

Probably every *New Thought* writer has begun research first by reading McTaggert's book. She introduces "The Field" ....similar to what Chopra refers to as "pure potentiality." She presents the hard evidence of what spiritual masters have taught us for centuries.

39. Morrissey, Mary Manin (Editor). (2002). *New Thought: A Practical Spirituality. New York:* Tarcher/Putnam.

Once called an "alternative spirituality," New Thought got its start with the attention to the transcendentalists authors and thinkers of the mid-19th century. Founded by Phineas Parkhurst Quimby, the philosophy was explored and expanded upon by some of the greatest minds of his and subsequent generations such as Ralph Waldo Emerson, Henry David Thoreau, Charles & Myrtle Fillmore, Ernest Holmes and others. This book is a series of essays in 5 genres from contemporary authors of New Thought in health, prosperity, creative endeavors, relationships and spiritual life.

40. Nabhaniilananda, Dada (2006). *Close Your Eyes & Open Your Mind: An Introduction to spiritual meditation*. Waitsfield, Vermont: InnerWorld Publications.

One of the best spiritual primers I have ever read. His clear and concise explanations of spiritual meditation is enlightening and beautifully inspiring, free of jargon, and masterfully delivered. The wisdom in this little book is cased in practicality and is destined to become one of the prized books in your spiritual collection.

41. Newton, Michael, (1994). *Journey of Souls, Case Studies of Life Between Lives*. St. Paul, Minnesota: Llewellyn Publications.

Newton, a noted hypnotherapist/psychologist, has developed a technique to reach his subjects hidden memories of the hereafter. He shares the story of 29 of his subjects as they describe the "space between lives" and previous incarnations. As they reveal graphic details of those lives, Newton prods them to share what the spirit world is really like, where we go and what we do as souls, and why we choose to come back in certain bodies.

42. Newton, Michael. (2000). *Destiny of Souls, New Case Studies of Life Between Lives*. Woodbury, MN: Llewellyn Publications.

> *Destiny of Souls* is a continuance of Newton's studies (67 more) since his previous book. Here his subjects reveal, in deep hypnosis, our purpose on earth, spiritual settings where souls go after death, soul mates, spirit guides, why we chose certain bodies and more. This book is designed for those who are new to afterlife studies and for readers of Newton's previous best seller listed above.

43. Rasha, (2003). *Oneness*. Santa Fe, New Mexico: Earthstar Press.

> If there is one book that comprehensively presents a direct path to one's own God realization, it is this one. Filled with incredible metaphysical concepts, Rasha's work is unprecedented in her profound dialogue with "universal presence." Her divine revelations gifts us with astounding visions of who we really are and where we're heading.

44. Rinpoche, Sogyal (1992) Edited by Andrew Harvey & Patrick Gaffney. *The Tibetan Book of Living and Dying*. San Francisco: HarperSanFrancisco.

> A priceless resource of Tibetan Buddhism that gives practical instruction and spiritual guidance on how to live in light of the greatest teacher of all—death. This book is a clear-eyed look at the profound insights of the "Bardo," or process of death. A book that is a "must have" in your library for consultation and reference.

45. Sha, Zhi Gang (2006) *Soul Mind Body Medicine*, Novato, California: New World Library.

> What is the real secret to healing? Dr. Zhi Gang Sha shows that love and forgiveness are the golden keys to soul healing. Trained as a Western medical doctor in China, Sha practices traditional Chinese medicine in China and North America. This book includes healing methods for over 100 ailments from the common cold to back pain to heart disease to diabetes. A great handbook for anyone to take control of their own healing.

46. Simon, Sidney B. (1990). *Forgiveness: How to Make Peace With Your Past and Get on With Your Life*. New York: Warner Books, Inc.

> Dr. Simon of *Values Clarification* fame which captured the 60s, 70s and 80s writes a lovely little book dealing only with the subject of forgiveness. He cites many examples and writes about how one can understand and appreciate the power and attitude of loving forgiveness.

47. Singh, Kirpal (2000). *Prayer* (6th Edition) California: Ruhani Satsang, Divine Science of the Soul.

> Prayers of the world from all faiths, modern and ancient, is the subject of this book written by a spiritual master in the spiritual lineage of Guru Nanek, the Sikh ascended master. The Master Singh, who led worldwide initiations onto the path of Ruhani Satsang, talks about the meaning of prayer and how it is delivered and received. His definition of what a prayer is and should be is uplifting and truly inspirational.

48. Stone, Joshua David (1999). *Soul Psychology.* New York: Random House

> Stone has a spiritual center in San Diego and a daily force who explains the factors of psychology as it relates to the soul. This book is full of wonderful charts, thoughts and practices for all of us to examine. He also explains and examines how spiritual "rays" affect us.

49. Stone, Joshua David (1994). *The Complete AscensionManual.* Flagstaff, Arizona: Light Technology Publishing.

> A manual of how to achieve ascension in this lifetime. Stone brings it all, from our spiritual history in Lemuria and Atlantis to how we can utilize these historical lessons to actively begin the work of our own unique ascension to the superconsciousness. He provides a myriad of techniques that any one of us can address and practice. In addition, he provides a list of 147 "golden keys" to achieving liberation and ascension in this lifetime.

50. Tolle, Eckhart (2005). *A New Earth: Awakening to Your Life's Purpose.* New York: Plume/Penguin.

> This book was a featured telecast over several weeks with Oprah Winfrey. He expounds on the NOW and gives us new insights into our soul as well as how to become connected to the indestructible essence in our being. A highly readable, enjoyable, and thoughtful book.

51. Tolle, Eckhart (1999). *The Power of Now: A Guide to Spiritual Enlightenment.* Novato, California: New World Publishing and Vancouver, B.C.: Namaste Publishing.

> Tolle writes extensively on the NOW, the presence that dwells with us. It is in this NOW that our soul actually is able to communicate with the Source. He suggests that we will need to leave our analytical mind and its false created self, the ego, behind. He uses simple language and a question and answer format to guide the reader.

52. Walsch, Neale Donald (1996). *Conversations With God: An Uncommon Dialogue (Book 1)*. New York: Putnam.

> Suppose you could ask God the most puzzling questions about existence—questions about love and faith, life and death, good and evil. Suppose God provided clear, understandable answers. It happened to Neale Donald Walsch — an incredible revelation that will open your inner eye and soul. It is truly a conversation with God. This was the book that jolted my wife, Annie Elizabeth, into another world.

53. Williamson, Marianne (1992). *A Return to Love*. New York: HarperCollins.

> A lovely, lovely book. Marianne, in beautifully human terms, describes the lessons taught in *A Course in Miracles*. Her engaging and uncomplicated writing will thrill the reader as she relates her own spiritual journey as she ponders the magical thoughts contained in the teachings of the book. This book is so well written and so clearly understandable, that I recommend that it be read by everyone who is on a spiritual quest. Marianne has several books published now and leads seminars all over the country with her uncommon wisdom.

54. Wilson, A.N. (1992). *Jesus: A Life*. New York: W.W. Norton & Co.

> What are the facts about the life of Jesus as opposed to the myths, or unprovable tenets of faith surrounding the miracles, death and resurrection? ...So much more in this daring and unconventional, and scholarly book.

55. Wolf, Dr. Fred Alan (2005). *Dr. Quantum: A User's Guide to Your Universe*. (6 CD Set) Boulder, Colorado: Sounds True.

> Matter can move backwards and forwards in time. Objects may be in two places at once. Simply looking at an event can alter it instantaneously. These are the type of phenomenal questions that "Dr. Quantum" answers...and he does it with clarity, humor and scholarship. This six C.D. set is a wonderfully entertaining romp in the world of quantum physics. Just plug it in to your CD player, relax and enjoy. You'll love it!

56. Yogananda, Paramahansa (1946). *The Autobiography of a Yogi*. Los Angeles, California: Self-Realization Fellowship.

> Have you ever wondered what a spiritual Yogi goes through in his/her quest for enlightenment? This sensational book thrilled the nation in the 1960s. Yogananda was one of the first Hindu gurus who set up his

mission and ashram in the West. His work here influenced many to begin their own spiritual quest. His ashram is thriving in Southern California.

57. Yogananda, Paramahansa (1988). *Where There Is Light: Insight and Inspiration for Meeting Life's Challenges.* Los Angeles, California: Self-Realization Fellowship.

A wonderful compilation of thoughts by the Master. This is the kind of book you can "dip" into at any point and gain incredible insight in a host of spiritual subjects. Yogananda writes in an engaging, easy to relate to manner.

58. Zukav, Gary (1979). *The Dancing Wu Li Masters.* New York: Bantam Books.

O.K. Here is another "wow" book that is so well done that it becomes a top notch "must read." Zukav is a master at explaining in simple language that we non-physicists are able to understand regarding the wonders of quantum physics. He adeptly and clearly shows the magnitude of the early discoveries of Issac Newton while highlighting the contrasts of the "old physics" and the quantum leap in the attempt to understand the "new physics." Don't miss this book!

59. Zukav, Gary (1989). *The Seat of the Soul.* New York: Simon & Schuster.

One of my favorite books! If you are searching for meanings of life and our part in it, Zukav presents it all in a very easy to follow format loaded with logical and spiritual meanderings. Well worth making it one of the first books you read.

CPSIA information can be obtained
at www.ICGtesting.com
Printed in the USA
FSHW01n1914010918
51716FS

9 781935 914075